**W9-DHM-695**

# TEACHING YOUR CHILD TO MAKE DECISIONS

**Also by Gordon Porter Miller**

*After High School*
*Decisions and Outcomes* (co-author)
*How to Decide: A Guide for Women*
*It's Your Business to Decide*
*Life Choices*
*Test Yourself: A Career Quiz Book*

# Teaching Your Child to Make Decisions

## HOW TO RAISE A RESPONSIBLE CHILD

by Gordon Porter Miller
with Bob Oskam

HARPER & ROW, PUBLISHERS, New York
Cambridge, Philadelphia, San Francisco, London
1817  Mexico City, São Paulo, Sydney

FIRST EDITION

*Designer: Sidney Feinberg*

---

Library of Congress Cataloging in Publication Data
Miller, Gordon Porter.
   Teaching your child to make decisions.
   Includes index.
   1. Child rearing.   2. Decision making in children—Study and teaching.
3. Child development.   I. Oskam, Bob.   II. Title.
HQ772.M4442   1984       649'.1       83-48370
ISBN 0-06-038033-0

---

84 85 86 87 88 10 9 8 7 6 5 4 3 2 1

To all those parents who have taken the time to help their children learn to decide so that they might lead productive and responsible lives today and tomorrow

# Contents

# Acknowledgments

Decisionmaking is a skill that can be learned and practiced and improved over time. But it takes courage and a real commitment to decisionmaking to bring about the kind of learning that is possible.

To this end, I want to thank the hundreds of parents, teachers, counselors, and children who gave me an opportunity to share my ideas with them and who were willing to try these concepts with others. It was only through their efforts that solid activities and examples were able to be developed.

My wife, Heide, has been invaluable in generating new and improved ways to use decision concepts with young people, especially our children, who have been a genuine pleasure to grow up with.

Finally, this book was a long time in reaching publication. If it were not for Bob Oskam's creative ideas and editorial assistance it might not have made it.

—GORDON PORTER MILLER

In working on this book, I've more than ever come to appreciate the love shown me by my parents, Teunis and Isabella Oskam, in their efforts to prepare me for a happily independent and productive life of my own.

I owe particular thanks to Maryanne Colas, whose enthusiasm and support were instrumental in my taking on this project, and to Helen Moore and Carol Cohen of Harper & Row, who were unwavering in their support and patience throughout the months it took to complete the manuscript.

My collaboration with Dr. Gordon Porter Miller has proven an enjoyable growth experience. I am richer for having had the opportunity to share in the presentation of principles and techniques that offer valuable aid in preparing a next generation to meet the challenges that life sets us all. And I feel fortunate to have been able to work with a collaborator who has continually responded to my efforts with warm encouragement and honest appreciation.

—BOB OSKAM

# Introduction: Choices and Consequences—Why Bother?

To see the importance of teaching children how to make decisions requires only a moment's reflection on the importance of decisionmaking in your own life.

The shape of your life is a result of choices made. You are certain to be able to recall events and decisions that have had an impact on who and what you've turned out to be. Sometimes these events were decisions you made consciously for yourself. In other cases they represented choices that others made for you or imposed upon you. In either situation, the action taken affected what you were subsequently prepared for or unprepared for, what you were afterward able or not able to do.

Oh, you may at once protest, my life has been shaped by circumstance. I am who I am and what I am in consequence of forces and influences beyond my control. My parents decreed the values and goals I should strive after. My teachers required me to follow preset patterns of social interaction. Economic position limited the opportunities for self-development. Society at large restricts the extent to which I can express myself as an individual.

Yes, certainly you are somewhat a product of circumstance. You have been and are subjected to pressures from the world

1

around you. There is no escape from those. You cannot spin a cocoon to isolate yourself from your environment while you change into the who or what you'd ideally like to be.

But you do have, and have had, the capacity to choose your response to the world around you. You couldn't choose your parents, but now you're an adult; you can choose to accept or reject values and goals they pushed you toward. You had to accept your teachers, but it was and is your choice to further explore or apply the lessons they taught you. You may be far from the economic status you dream of, but it's up to you whether and how to pursue that dream. And as for society, you can support its values and structure, you can passively acquiesce to them, or you can work for change—the decision is up to you.

These choices confront you every day. The pattern of response you've developed to them has already come to define who and what you are. Consider simply the role in which you're approaching this book, that of a parent. It's as a result of decisions you've made that you're even in this role—decisions about whom to go out with, whom to marry, and whether or not to take on family responsibilities.

### THERE'S NO ESCAPE

You are continually faced with decisions. There's no avoiding them. You make them whether you realize it or not, whether you want to or not. And every decision carries a consequence or consequences with it.

You cannot avoid consequences by sitting still, by refusing to make a decision when one is possible or called for. Your refusal to choose is a decision, too, and it carries consequences of its own with it. Rejecting any choice between available courses of action subjects you to the consequences of inaction. You may try to avoid the risks attached to taking action. However, you cut yourself off from possible opportunities for gain as well, and you subject yourself to whatever the failure to risk carries with it.

Imagine you are sitting at home watching television with your family. You smell something—an acrid, burning odor. Do you get up to investigate? Do you just sit there and reassure yourself it's nothing? In either case, what you do is the result of a decision, and either decision carries with it its own set of risks and consequences. In this particular situation, deciding to do nothing may very easily expose you and those you love to greater eventual risk and more severe negative consequences than deciding to investigate.

Life situations are not all as clear-cut as the threat of a house on fire. It's easier to imagine or pretend that passively going along with the tide of everyday events frees you of any need to worry about risks or consequences you might otherwise expose yourself to. But what about the risk you'll prove unable to cope when events work out to your disadvantage? What about the opportunities lost through your decision not to pursue possibilities actively?

Think about it. You're a parent. That means the risks and consequences attached to what you do or fail to do extend beyond yourself. They affect the character and direction of your child's life, too. His or her happiness as well as your own is inextricably linked to the outcome of decisions you make on a daily basis, to how you respond to whatever choices are available.

You make decisions every day. You have to. Naturally you hope they're the right ones. Often you convince yourself they are, even though you may have developed no means of weighing choices open to you, even though you may have only a vague sense of consequences beyond the short range. There's no prescription for every combination of circumstances you face. You have to choose your own response. That's a serious responsibility when you think of the potential effect on your life in any instance. It's doubly serious when you take into account that your decisions have tremendous impact on the lives of others who are dear to you.

It goes beyond that. Even if you're relatively satisfied with the choices you make both for yourself and for your children, the fact is you can't carry the ball for both forever. Your children will inevitably face choices of their own on their own. There's no way you can oversee every decision that faces them.

A mother recently assured me she recognized how important it was to teach her child how to decide. "But," she added, "I plan to make all of my child's decisions until she's in the eighth grade." She failed altogether to take into account the reality that children are already making choices of their own long before then.

While a parent will reasonably feel it appropriate to make decisions for children in areas that are beyond their capacity for understanding, it is folly to ignore the many decisions children routinely make for themselves by the time they are in the third grade. All kinds of decisions—life-shaping decisions—are being faced and acted upon very early in life, a lot earlier than most parents would like to admit. Consider, for example, that an orientation toward occupation develops as early as the third grade. Sex role stereotypes are being established. Patterns of behavior are already assuming a fixed character. Did you know that eventual high school dropouts can be identified with considerable accuracy by the time students reach the fourth grade?

Not only is it impossible for you to escape making decisions that have an impact on your life and that of your children, it's impossible as well to shield them from the need to make decisions of their own before you deem them prepared. Their decisions also lead to consequences, including some with long-range implications influencing the course of life in later years.

So your task as parent is twofold: first, to ensure the decisions you make for yourself and for your family lead to consequences that provide benefit for both; second, to provide your children a framework for approaching choices presented so that decisions they make contribute to rather than detract from their chances for happiness.

### THE PAYOFF

A recent study identified four key elements in what happiness means to people: involvement, control, freedom, and the sense of doing something worthwhile. I find these elements exactly descriptive of the payoffs available to those who learn to make good decisions.

As a parent, you want that payoff for your children, too. During their early years, they are wholly dependent on you. As they mature, the model you present as a decisionmaker greatly influences the approach they take to situations offering a choice among alternatives. (Let's be clear that that's what a decision is—a choice among alternatives. No decision is required unless more than one course of action is possible.) Mastering and passing along a systematic approach to decision-making will do more than anything else to put the payoffs within reach, both for you and for those you love.

### *Involvement*

A decision requires a definition of yourself. Establishing a sense of direction under any circumstances necessitates knowing where you're starting from and what you're starting with. You become involved because you're part of the process. You have a say about what is happening to you. That does not mean you somehow become able to predict the future. It means you have an input into what the future turns out to be.

Those who seek to avoid making choices sacrifice a definition of self. They permit others to shape their lives; they deprive themselves of the opportunity for involvement. You see people like this all around you—people maintaining personal relationships, getting married, having children only because of passively going along with others' expectations. Typically, the aftermath of this noninvolvement is marked by a lack of personal satisfaction in the life led.

This is enough of a tragedy for the individual who surrenders self to the expectations of others. In a family context it makes for a double tragedy. Noninvolved parents not only severely limit their own potential satisfaction, they maintain an environment limiting that possibility for their children, too. In setting and reinforcing a passive role model, they discourage development in their children of the kind of initiative that leads to a defined sense of self. The result? In some cases a pathetic passing on of an approach to life that stresses only conformity to what outside authority figures appear to mandate. In others an explosive rebellion, because children resentfully reject taking their place in a society they see as having given them no say in their own future.

### *Control*

Decision implies action. Follow-through along any line of endeavor requires a commitment of resources on the part of the decider. Since your resources are always in some way limited—by time, money, effort required, etc.—the idea is to make them count. You do that by exercising control. It's by skillful assessment and employment of resources that you ensure or improve the chance of success in achieving goals you've set yourself.

You'll never have absolute control. A good decision can lead to poor results. Circumstance does play a role in what is or is not possible. For example, it takes a college degree to be more sure of an eventual good-paying job, but many recent college graduates find it difficult to get a job at all. That doesn't mean their decision to attend college was necessarily less than wise. A good decision improves the odds, it doesn't guarantee the results.

However, developing a capacity for making good decisions

provides you something of a cushion as far as results go. It gives you an enhanced ability to cope with results, whatever they may be. Learning to weigh your options and gauge your next move still provides you some control over how you will be affected by setbacks. Control means never settling passively into the role of victim even though you experience setbacks. And at one time or other everyone experiences those.

Nurturing the capacity for independent decisionmaking in your children provides them a foundation for self-confident movement into the future. It encourages a realistic awareness of resource limitations. At the same time it prompts creativity in the employment of whatever resources are available.

Providing children the skill for exercising control over their lives is also crucial for their developing a sense of responsibility. Children learn to see that their actions bring consequences. They learn that a choice between alternatives is also a decision to risk or bear whatever consequences attach to their choice. They come to see a connection between their actions and what happens to them subsequently. It's a sad commentary on the incidence of failure in this area to see so many dissatisfied young adults all around us holding others totally and forever responsible for both who are what they are and for who and what they ever will be.

### Freedom

A practiced decisionmaking ability increases the flexibility you have for response to the world around you. It increases your freedom by opening your eyes to the wide range of alternatives that lie continually before you. It enables you to look beyond the obvious, and the best chance of getting what one wants comes to the person who has done a good job of looking beyond the obvious. That person stands the greatest chance of surmounting limitations that otherwise restrict opportunity. And that's what freedom is about.

This concept of freedom is of major importance for parents.

Children typically view freedom as a matter of license to select among the choices they see and the consequences they hope for. One of the main problems for children—and one especially pronounced with adolescents—is an inability as yet to identify all the alternatives available in a given situation or realistically to project all likely consequences, particularly over the long term. Giving in to their demand for freedom can actually have the effect of limiting their flexibility of response to the world around them. They do not learn to consider all the options that may exist; they do not learn to anticipate consequences beyond those they expect. They paradoxically lose their freedom just when they think they've achieved it.

Parents who insist on an evaluation of broader possibilities with respect to available alternatives and potential consequences promote freedom at the very time it seems they restrict it. They do more to ensure their children the best chance of actually getting what they want over the long term, or as close to that as is possible. Teaching children the way to go about making considered decisions means requiring them to weigh choices and consequences so there's less chance of being surprised in a negative, limiting way.

## A Sense of Doing Something Worthwhile

Taking the initiative in choosing among alternatives available in any set of circumstances always ensures that what you do has a direct personal relevance. You focus on your own goals instead of following those set by others. You pursue what you see to be your own potential and, in so doing, consciously take a hand in your own growth as an individual. What you do automatically takes on a deeper personal significance, since what you want and hope and dream becomes an intrinsic factor in everything you do. You see meaning in what you undertake. Every action has the promise of accomplishing something worthwhile.

In contrast, "not deciding" is the most certain route to getting stuck with life's leftovers, and these rarely add up to something worthwhile.

Teaching children how to decide enables them to find meaning in what they do, too. You provide them a framework for affirming personal values, for pursuing personal goals. They come to see choices beyond the "leftovers" of the preceding generation. (An added benefit is that they better understand the decisions you've made or make that affect them, even if there may still be some element of disagreement about those.) Instead of complaining of an empty, purposeless existence, they learn to move ahead with their own sense of direction. They come to a recognition that opportunities continually arise for introducing desirable change into their relationship with the world around them. As they mature, they achieve a means for taking charge of their own lives in a positive way.

### YOUR TASK AS PARENT

The simple fact that you are a parent means that you have a responsibility that extends beyond yourself. Whether or not you think in terms of your children's long-range future, both social convention and explicit laws of social order set you the task of supervising their emergence into adulthood. You have a primary role in preparing them for independence.

You probably realize this. Most likely you've taken on this responsibility willingly, or at least you think you have. Many of today's parents think their task well done merely in the provision of a reasonably secure home environment, one in which food, shelter, and clothing are provided and in which there's a caring emotional involvement with the children. Certainly those are essential for children's well-being. Yet in family after family you see those elements in place without the result being the emergence of responsible young adults willing and able to make their own way in the world. The children's needs in the area of learning to make decisions have been overlooked or ignored.

Most people will agree that learning to make good choices is vital and that one must expect to "pay" the consequences stemming from a willful action. But there is little evidence that much more than lip service is being generated when it comes to the decisionmaking needs of children.

In terms of learning the process, there are few courses in how to make choices. In fact, often when a young person, through whatever set of circumstances, does question decisions in the home or in the school, he or she is viewed as a troublemaker. Helping children learn to decide is threatening to many adults because it means more questions are going to be asked about the way things are done. It also poses the threat of conflict. The increasingly independent child invariably wants to assert initiative in areas of responsibility the parent may not yet be prepared to give over to him or her.

As a parent, it may appear you are giving up control of your children when you help them learn to decide. This may well occasion some anxiety for you.

But then think. Your children can no more escape having to make decisions than you can, even though you might wish you could somehow supervise all their choices until they're "of age." You might as well accept this reality.

And then think about the payoffs that exist for those who learn what decisionmaking is all about. Aren't those the very things you want your children to experience in life? Don't you want to prevent their happiness from being compromised by a passive attitude toward the world around them? Wouldn't you prefer they not suffer the results of a failure to recognize the consequences of their own actions? Wouldn't you rather they learned to evaluate available choices to their own advantage?

The task has already been set you. Like it or not, you have a choice to make—not whether you will take on the responsibility, but how you will fulfill the responsibility you already have.

This book should make the choice an easier one for you, directing you to a framework for action that leads to positive outcomes. Your children can't avoid decisions, so they might as well learn how to take the initiative. They might as well apply the techniques available for picking the alternative that's best out of those available. Providing them a reliable approach to life's choices is a major part of your job as a parent.

But it's not a job that ultimately provides benefit only to your children. You have to master the decisionmaking process yourself first. And as you develop competence as a decision-maker, you'll find it easier to identify short- and long-term consequences for yourself in any situation offering a choice between possible lines of action. It will be through the personal experience of the benefits good decisionmaking provides that you'll gain the insights that make it possible to pass the ability on to your children. It's truly a case of learning to help others through learning to help yourself.

The material that follows is given in three parts.

Part One, "A Brief Course in Decisionmaking," first explains what goes into any decision. A series of seven short lessons leads you to mastery of a proven technique for getting the best you can out of any situation.

Part Two, "Your Family Situation and Home Environment," outlines the characteristics in both parents and the home environment that contribute to teaching decisionmaking. There's particular emphasis on learning to recognize and manage differences. The information in these chapters applies whether you are the parent of a very young child or of a teenager.

Part Three, "Parenting Toward Independence," follows you through the stages of growth you will experience with your children. Depending on your child's age and level of maturity, you can expect to encounter certain situations more regularly. You will have to adjust your approach according to each child's ability to absorb information and apply it to his or her own situation.

Your aim in picking up this book is very likely to ensure you do the best you can to prepare your children for the issues and uncertainties of life. I'll show you how you can provide them that preparation. As a bonus, you'll also learn how to approach the issues and uncertainties of your own life with confidence, aside from your role as parent.

# PART I

# A Brief Course in Decisionmaking

---

Each of the chapters in this section comprises a lesson in decisionmaking. You will find your mastery of the techniques given more assured if you take the time to work through each lesson carefully as presented. A good approach is to take one chapter per day for study and review. In a week's time, you will be thoroughly familiar with what it takes to be a good decisionmaker.

# 1

# There Is a "Right" Approach

How do you make a good decision? If that's what you plan to teach your child, you have better first be sure you know what's involved.

Children commonly follow one of three patterns when it comes to making decisions. Sad to say, many adults never get far past those patterns either. Before we go into describing what makes for intelligent choices, let's see what to beware of. You might occasionally fall into a faulty approach yourself without realizing it, and to the extent you do, that compromises your ability and credibility when it comes to providing your children guidance.

## POOR DECISIONMAKING APPROACHES

### Doing the First Thing That Comes to Mind

This is a quick-reaction approach. You're faced with a situation that's uncomfortable or unexpected, and you respond without any thought other than to get out from under the threat of conflict or discomfort. Someone behaves in a manner you find disagreeable; you retaliate. Someone pushes you; you push back. Or maybe you run away. Whatever it is, you don't think; you act on impulse.

Sometimes doing the first thing that comes to mind proves appropriate. Generally it doesn't. Often the result is like jumping out of the frying pan into the fire, particularly in response to a problem situation. Rather than getting a solution, you aggravate the problem. Your reaction is something you commit yourself to with no meaningful thought given to consequences. So the result of what you do is as likely to be negative as positive.

### The "Me First" Action

"Me first" decisions involve more thought than doing the first thing that comes to mind, and to that extent they may be something of an improvement. But the improvement is only relative. The decisions reached are commonly short-sighted, and the consequences are likely to be unsatisfactory.

It's characteristic for those taking a "me first" approach to focus primarily on what is obviously desirable or fun at the moment. Actions taken reflect strictly personal needs and wants. There's no effort to consider their impact on others. The objective is always immediate self-gratification, and if that's at someone else's expense . . . well, who's got time to worry about what anybody else wants or needs?

Certainly it's sensible to consider self-interest when it comes to deciding on a course of action. But if you behave as though you were alone on the planet, you wind up complicating things for yourself even as you follow what seems an easy approach to making choices.

The fact is, you live in a social environment and do have to interact with others. When it becomes evident to others that you aren't concerned with their interests, you can bet they will stop taking yours into account. Then, to the extent you look to or depend on others for satisfaction of your wants and needs, you will find that more difficult to achieve. You'll never be alone on this planet, but you may end up feeling very alone.

### Looking Only to the Immediate Consequences

This is a better decisionmaking approach than the previous two, but again, that's only a relative distinction. The improvement is that consequences are considered and other people's interests taken into account as well as one's own. It's not enough of an improvement, since the consequences considered are only the immediate ones. There's no taking into account what could happen over the long term, no considering the long-range potential for damage to one's self-interest and for the interest of others. This is a common approach among teenagers (although there are plenty of adults who follow it, too).

Your high school–age daughter, Katherine, decides to stick as much as possible with some nonacademic course because she doesn't like the more academic subjects offered. Katherine figures her decision won't keep her from enjoying the social life of the school. Probably she'll have more time for that. Katherine is pretty sure her parents will raise no objection, since they're leaving it up to her to decide whether or not she wants to go to college.

What Katherine fails to take into account is that setting herself an easy course through school also closes off opportunities she might later find attractive. Once she's out of high school, she may be faced with having to go to work and having only limited skills to offer, living off her parents because she can't find work, or possibly rushing into marriage because that seems one of the few options open to her.

Everybody has experience with each of these approaches to decisionmaking. There's a sort of natural chronology we all go through. As very young children, we start by doing whatever comes to mind first in a situation. Then there's a phase during which we focus primarily on our own wants or needs while naively oblivious to the wants and needs of others. Once we see a clearer connection between cause and effect and realize the impact others can have on our lives, we start to think in terms both of consequences and of the effect of our actions upon those around us. The final step is thinking ahead to possible long-range consequences. But that's a mighty big step, and the average person finds it a very difficult one.

Most people will tell you that they take the long term into account in making decisions. However, press them on exactly how they do so, and you will find there's generally little sense of method involved. That's not to say they never make good decisions, but it does suggest something of a hit-or-miss approach to many situations that require making choices, particularly situations that are at all complex, as many important life decisions are.

Ironically, just when it's most important that all the variables—possibilities and probabilities—be carefully weighed and evaluated, the lack of a methodical approach sees some people choosing their actions in much the way children will. They do what comes to mind first, on the argument that it's best to follow your first intuition. They do a "me first" choice, figuring that that way whoever loses, it won't be they. Or, unclear about how to project long-range consequences, they opt for the most attractive short-range consequence. Are they confident of the decision reached? More likely they are simply hoping for the best.

Confidence from standing up for an action comes from knowing how to make a good decision, from feeling you have followed sound procedures in reaching the choice made. To be confident, you have to face the future squarely, doing all you can to assess the impact of every choice possible—*after you've done all you can to see what is possible.* You're dealing with the unknown as well as the known. That's why following a systematic approach is so important—so you can eliminate as many of the question marks as possible, so you can get the best sense of what risks you face in any situation.

## A FRAMEWORK FOR GOOD DECISIONS

Take a moment to think of important decisions you've made in your life: career choice, marriage, having a family, establishing a home.

Do you recall how you went about them? Did you recognize these events as decisions, or did they just seem to happen to you somehow? What part did the actions or expectations of others play in moving you to whatever it is you did in these areas?

If you can clearly recall any of these situations, jot down what things you took into consideration. Once you've worked out as complete a list as you can, review briefly just what you did in taking each into consideration. Then try to re-create the order of steps you took in reaching your decision. Use the space provided on page 20 for this decision inventory.

It's more than likely you have only a vague sense of what you did in taking some of the considerations listed into account. Possibly there are considerations you can now see as important that you overlooked altogether at the time. And what luck did you have in trying to remember the order in which you approached and dealt with each item of importance on this list?

This simple decision inventory will provide you a graphic illustration of your own pattern up to now in making decisions. Do you in fact see a pattern? Or are you nonplussed to discover you don't? Most people don't. How, then, do they go about teaching their children the basics of an intelligent, reliable approach to life's choices?

Fortunately, there is a reliable framework for making good decisions: one that will work for you in whatever circumstances face you, and one that will serve the needs of your children. It's an easy-to-remember seven-step process following a sequence you will quickly recognize as natural.

*1.* Establish your *values.*

*2.* Set your *goals.*

*3.* Identify possible action *alternatives.*

*4.* Collect *information* on all possibilities.

*5.* Look ahead to *consequences* and how they can be managed.

*6.* Take responsible *action,* the best alternative for you.

*7. Review* the action taken.

There, in a nutshell, is how you go about making good decisions. Study this framework briefly to fix each step in mind. Copy the list onto a separate piece of paper to post somewhere in easy view. That will help you.

**Decision:** _____

| Things I Considered | What I Did Upon Consideration of Them | Order of Activity in Movement to Decision |
|---|---|---|
| 1. | | |
| 2. | | |
| 3. | | |
| 4. | | |
| 5. | | |
| 6. | | |
| 7. | | |
| 8. | | |
| 9. | | |
| 10. | | |
| 11. | | |
| 12. | | |

*(Use a separate sheet if you need more space.)*

These seven steps—think "lucky seven"—are the key to improving the odds in your and your children's favor whenever it comes to the opportunities you have every day for making life a rewarding growth experience. They are, at the same time, the key to controlling negativity that might otherwise move in on you unexpectedly.

# 2

# Establish What's Important to You—Values

One of the biggest problems in making decisions and in helping children decide is confusion with regard to values.

A value is *a quality or characteristic you hold in high esteem*. It is a standard for judging something desirable or undesirable, important or unimportant.

Whenever you face a choice, the natural first question to ask yourself is: What is important to me? Everything else flows from that—how you set your goals, why you prefer one alternative over another, how you assess the risks involved in any action, how you rate the results of the action taken.

At first sight, that seems simple enough. However, there's a complicating reality: Nobody pursues just one value at a time. Everyone has his or her own set of values—*in the plural*—and they rarely dovetail neatly into one another. They rarely make for one easily defined set of priorities you can quickly apply to any set of circumstances.

You can provide yourself a very quick answer in any situation to the question of what's important. That won't necessarily mean you've established all the values you really want taken into account. More likely, you've only jumped at the first one you saw or wanted to consider.

What about values across a broader perspective?

Look at the sample list below. Each of the entries is a common value that you may very well share. Put a check (✔) next to those you feel are important.

| | | |
|---|---|---|
| Independence | Privacy | Mobility |
| Financial security | Belief in God | Honesty |
| Physical health | Loyalty | Recognition |
| A sense of achievement | Appearance | Creativity |
| Emotional balance | Education | Helping others |
| Companionship | Reputation | Comfort |
| Convenience | Culture | Togetherness |

The list isn't necessarily complete; you will probably be able to identify other values important to you. But just in looking at this list, you can see something of the range of possibilities. And it doesn't take much to imagine situations in which one value somewhat clashes with another.

You can see that establishing values involves both recognizing those that come into play and developing a clear sense of priorities among them. You don't want to overlook values important to you, because that immediately compromises your chances of satisfaction in what you do. But because some conflict is always likely, to assure maximum satisfaction you do have to determine which is/are most important to you.

It takes some skill to make this determination. First you have to know what is important to you. Then you have to establish preferences in each case so that the eventual action taken reflects and accommodates those things you cherish most. That is a three-step sequence: a move from (1) *acceptance* (this is important) to (2) *preference* (this is more important) to (3) *action* (this is important enough to do something about).

Unfortunately, most people have little experience in spelling out their values. At best they have a vague awareness of concepts like traditional family values, security, job satisfaction, friendship, and happiness. However, these are inevitably so vague that the prospective decisionmaker does not know what they really mean. The result is bound to be confusion.

How do you establish priorities between generalities like these? You can't. For one thing, there's too much overlap. For another, what exactly goes into concepts like job satisfaction varies widely from person to person. You've got to be more specific.

### ESTABLISH YOUR PREFERENCES

Take a moment to look back at the common values listed. Note in particular the values you checked off as important to you. Are they really important *to you?*

Most people have some difficulty here. You commonly find they check off values they feel expected to honor as well as those that really are personal to them.

Values are learned. They come to us from a variety of sources: parents, peers, religious teachings, school, personal experiences, and society in general. Learning values is a lifelong process.

Depending on how one's life unfolds and what one makes of that, values change. That gives rise to conflict within many people. They don't keep up with the change. They feel guilty about abandoning old values. They feel pressure from others to behave according to those values. Giving in to guilt and expectations, their actions aim to please others rather than please themselves. Did you, in checking off the values important to you, unconsciously check off any that you felt expected to honor but don't fully share?

Most of the values listed are probably quite acceptable to you. Perhaps you checked all of them as important to you and are perfectly satisfied that your selections truly are *your* selections. If so, fine. Just be sure they are.

But now, to the next task, separating the important from the most important—and remember that this means *most important to you.*

Try this. Write the number *1* next to the value that is most important to you, a *2* next to the second most important, and so on until you have ranked the top five values on this list. Now you're being forced to state your preferences.

You will probably find it something of a struggle to establish an absolute ranking between the values you hold. Because of the role values play in making decision, you'll undoubtedly experience something of the same struggle when it comes to choosing among several courses of action. Most actions cannot accommodate everything important to you to the degree you'd like. You have to know your preferences so you can make certain tradeoffs, with an eye to maximum satisfaction.

Examine your rankings once more. Try to imagine how you would have ranked these items ten years ago. It is perfectly reasonable to expect that some things that were once important to you have lost importance, while others have gained in importance as you've developed new needs and attitudes in life.

You can gain an additional insight into what is most important to you now by making a list of things you enjoy doing. Then try to determine what values are accommodated in those activities. For example, you may list "driving my car." The values you identify may be power, mobility, and independence; they may be prestige, adventure, and/or privacy. The important thing is that you begin to understand what makes the activity enjoyable. As you make a note of the values satisfied in different activities, you will probably find yourself repeating some more than others. Right there you have a good clue to where your actual preferences lie.

Here's another helpful exercise: Identify a person you think of as successful. (It can be someone living or dead, famous or relatively unknown.) What do you see reflected in that person's life that leads you to conclude he or she exemplifies your definition of success? Think in terms of specified values you can identify. Again, the list you come up with will help put your own preferences into sharper focus.

In either of these exercises, monitor your reactions. Did you feel any pressure to list a value others expect to see you upholding? If you did, make a note of that value on a separate sheet—even if you resisted the pressure to include it among your own. Values that wind up on that separate sheet will be those that you haven't fully accepted as your own. And decisions that involve those values may prove troublesome for you until you sort out your feelings about them.

Did a lot of possible choices come to mind? If so, how did you narrow these down when deciding *your* preferences?

Do you feel good about those you've indicated? Would you declare your choices publicly?

Did you think to include yourself when identifying a person you regard as successful?

All these are important questions to keep in mind as you come to conclusions about the values you want to see reflected in your decision.

At this point you probably see more clearly that conflict develops as you move from accepting values to establishing preferences among them. This conflict will become even more intense when you act on these values. Action assumes commitment. Up to now you've been engaging in an intellectual exercise. But you are not what you think; you are what you do. That's the bottom line in the real world of decisions. Of course, what you think influences what you do, but it's the doing that moves you forward or holds you back.

Look back to the decision inventory you filled out in the last chapter. Identify what values were instrumental in deciding on the action you ultimately took. What were some of the conflicts you experienced? How did you resolve those? Can you now see how you established your preferences, where you may have disregarded personal preferences in favor of others' expectations? As you've come to a clearer awareness of the values you hold now, do you find yourself thinking you'd approach that situation differently today?

It's vital to recognize that values and value preferences differ from person to person. Observing and accepting your own priorities is part of affirming your own individuality. Observing and accepting others' priorities as different from yours is integral to understanding why they do as they do. It's also a necessary part of helping others learn to decide. You can't realistically expect that teaching others to make good decisions means pushing them into following your value priorities. You may think the results satisfying because they'd satisfy you; they won't provide the person you mean to help the satisfaction he or she wants.

# 3

# Aim at Specific Objectives—Goals

Once you've come to grips with what is important to you, it is much easier to get moving toward something you tell yourself you want.

Identifying what you want in any area of life requires developing focus, establishing the line of direction in which to move. That's where goals come in. In setting goals, you project yourself into the future, defining the situation or circumstances you want to see realized within a given time frame. That can be very specific—by next Saturday, for example. Or you can leave it more or less open—sometime within the next couple months.

You're setting up a plan for change, looking to make real something that now exists only in your mind.

You start with where you are—this is your first reference point. You define where you want to be—that provides the second reference point. Your sense of direction grows out of seeing the distance you have to cover to get from the first to the second.

Many people have trouble setting and pursuing goals precisely because it requires stepping into the future. You will have to plot a course to follow from now on. And that seems to them to be limiting. Once you set a course to follow, as they

see it, you eliminate the chance of movement in other directions. As long as you don't set a course, the potential exists for
going anywhere.

There are two basic problems with this attitude.

First of all, it overlooks the inescapable fact that everyone
continually moves from one reality (the present) to a next reality (the future). Whether or not you set goals for yourself, the
fact of that movement alone affects what's possible. You can
never anchor yourself so that a perpetual, unlimited range of
potential remains open to you. A potential that exists for you
today could be gone tomorrow, without any initiative you've
taken having influenced its disappearance.

The other problem lies in the illusory nature of counting
potential as something already in hand. Potential refers to
some possibility of achievement, not to what already exists. To
reach for nothing because you don't want to choose among
possibilities means you never take a hand in making any of
those possibilities real. You simply drift passively along, holding onto fantasies about all that could happen or might happen, without exerting effort to increase chances that anything
will happen. You abdicate whatever chance you do have of
realizing possibilities that are attractive to you.

It is difficult to step into the future. Young people in particular find it uncomfortable. They see their struggle with the
present as enough to focus on. But setting and pursuing goals
is the only avenue for getting control in life and for making
your resources count. Otherwise you never get beyond just
trying to cope with life as it's handed to you on a day-to-day
basis. It's only by focusing on and moving ahead to something
you want that you improve your chances for becoming more
than a passive victim of your circumstances.

### FORMULATING GOAL STATEMENTS

Directed movement requires focused attention. The more
narrowly you can pinpoint your target, the better your

chances of being on target with any action you undertake. That means getting specific.

More often than not, people start off with nebulous descriptions of what they want in the future: "to be happy," "to work with people," "the best for my family," or something else along those lines. That kind of vagueness provides you the same difficulty that vagueness in identifying values presents. You can include a hundred different things within these generalities, not all of which will be compatible. It's like aiming at a fog bank instead of a clearly defined target. And the lack of clear vision is as likely to discourage action as it is to lead to any initiative.

Think of an objective you'd like to achieve. Let's work within the context of this book: let's suppose that your objective as you first think of it is "to help my child lead a more rewarding life." Sounds good, but what does that mean? It could mean any of a hundred things: seeing your child get into the right social set, making sure your child takes advantage of every educational opportunity available, helping your child into a well-paying job, and so on. In fact, the number of possible alternatives this leaves open is so overwhelming that choosing a line of action to follow is going to be very difficult. Unless you get more specific, a goal statement like this is as likely to lead to doing nothing as it is to lead to a meaningful program of assistance.

It's fine to start with a generality when it comes to working toward a goal statement, but a generality is not suitable as a goal statement. You have to boil it down to a specific. Only then does a line of action become apparent.

Consider this possible sequence for the vague statement we started with above:

"I want to help my child lead a more rewarding life."
"I want my child to be happy."
"I want my child to feel that life has meaning for him or her."

"I want my child to know what he or she wants and why he or she wants it."

"I want my child to make choices that satisfy him or her."

"I want my child to feel able to set his or her own course in life."

"I want my child to recognize opportunities for what they are."

"I want my child to know how to choose an alternative that provides him or her the best chance of getting what he or she wants."

"I want my child to know what goes into making good decisions."

"I want to help my child learn the decisionmaking process."

As you can see, it's not until you get down near the bottom of the list that a line of action starts to emerge. Only then is the goal stated specifically enough so that you have a reasonably clear sense of what to do.

When formulating goal statements, keep at it until you see that line of action emerge.

There is a word of warning to add, however: Once again, be sure you are following your priorities rather than those of people around you. Be sure it's your agenda you're following, not someone else's. If you allow confusion in this area, the value payoff will be less than adequate for you. You'll find yourself pursuing goals without enthusiasm (if you stick with them at all) or that there's no sense of satisfaction in achieving the goal. Note, for example, that a broad goal statement like "I want my child to be happy" can easily be boiled down to specifics in such fashion that others' expectations influence what line of action comes out at the end. You could, by equating happiness with social status, boil down to a line of action that meant sending your child to an expensive private school.

Generalities can be boiled down any number of ways. Don't take the approach that the bottom line somehow has to satisfy all the possibilities inherent in whatever vague sense of goal you start with. There's no way it can, for one thing. Also, don't get confused into thinking you are supposed to start with a generality and work your way down. It's much better to begin with specifics where these are apparent right away. But there is a way of moving yourself down from generalities if that's where you find yourself starting.

### VALUE PAYOFFS

People tend to go after something when they see a payoff in terms of values they hold. It's only common sense they won't commit to action if they don't at the same time see a projected return that in some way advances an interest they've identified as important.

There are two common problems to be alert to, however. One of these we've already twice identified: the tendency on your part to go after something others see as important rather than to follow your own priorities. But now view that problem from another perspective. Don't you sometimes have a tendency to want others to go after what you see as important rather than what they see as important? In your role as parent, there's great potential for difficulty and conflict here.

The other problem reflects back to the area of generalities. It's a frequent tendency to express goals more in terms of the long range than the tangible short range. Long-term goals are the easiest to set and the easiest to forget. After all, who's going to check up on something you said you wanted three years ago? And what sense of urgency are you going to feel today in taking directed action to meet a goal you've set three years into the future?

If you are truly serious about wanting to move in a given direction, it's a good idea to do something along the lines of getting more specific here. Break your long-term goal down into a series of steps—intermediate short-term goals. That way you recognize a more immediate payoff to be achieved. You find it easier to establish and maintain movement and to make timely adjustments as new information and developments come to light.

### GUIDELINES FOR SETTING GOALS

It's one thing to be aware of goal-setting problems. It's something else again to avoid getting tripped up by them. The following action-oriented suggestions should help you in your efforts to establish a sense of focus and direction for yourself and in trying to help others move from where they are today to where they'd like to be tomorrow.

*Start with small steps.* That will provide you a more immediate sense of progress. For example, a student might do better to set as a first objective improving by one letter grade in a particular course than immediately aiming at an overall B average for the term.

The idea is to devise intermediate steps that reinforce motivation and build confidence on the way to the more long-term objective.

*Set goals that appear within your reach.* You want to start with the notion that this is a "win" situation with regard to time, energy, skill, and the resources available.

*Make the start-up goal something you can measure.* Instead of saying "I want to lose weight," say "I want to lose two pounds by the end of the week." The measurability of an initial goal provides you more exact evidence for knowing when you've begun to achieve what you want.

*Build in time checks.* What progress do you expect to make in, say, two weeks' time? This gives you impetus. It also serves as a kind of honesty check—are you following through on what you want?—and tips you off to obstacles and/or the need to revise the initial goal statement.

*Give your goal focus.* While it is possible to go after several things at once, it's advisable to avoid either/or statements. A focused goal statement says that by such and such a time I'll do this, rather than by such and such a time I'll do this or that.

*Anticipate any possible obstacles,* even for short-term goals. Consider what might go wrong, what might get in the way of achieving your goal. It's basic to retaining the flexibility for possible adjustments that may prove necessary.

And in connection with that, keep in mind that goals are not cast in concrete. It is perfectly acceptable to revise or make adjustments in them along the way. After all, new information or new circumstances may call for some revision in your plan.

*Prepare for success!* It's important you have some preliminary notion of what you will have to do or expect to do once you reach your goal. What then? What of the new demands success will expose you to? You aren't going to stop dead in your tracks there, are you? If you do that you once again relinquish the control you can have over your destiny.

Look back again to the decision inventory you filled out in Chapter 1. Can you identify specific goals you had? Can you apply the guidelines developed here to plot out how you might have approached achieving any one of those? Or, if you'd rather start with a move into the future now, think in terms of something you'd like to achieve in the coming year.

### REACTIONS TO CHANGE

Whenever you act to realize a goal you've set for yourself, you initiate change. The change will have something of a ripple effect, giving rise to reactions that you'll do well to anticipate. You will particularly need to pay attention to negative reactions that could sabotage your goals. These can come from any of three sources.

## The Setting in Which You Are Operating

A new idea or action may affect the status quo of an organization or group you are part of or close to. Change along the lines you're following may threaten their comfortable existence. Your family, the department or company you work in, and/or the community may throw up roadblocks to impede your progress so that they don't have to adjust to a new situation they may see as disturbing.

## Individuals with Whom You Are in Regular Contact

Here, too, you may be threatening a comfortable status quo. Or regardless of what the status quo is, efforts at change may cause others to react with suspicion or anxiety. They may interpret your reaching for a goal as downgrading the role they play in your life or as setting up expectations of them as well.

Consider the example of the person who embarks on a weight loss program and then has to deal with Mom fixing a favorite dessert as a special treat just for him. Or think of the high school student who elects to get tutoring help after school and is razzed by classmates for brown-nosing the teacher. Sabotage of efforts to reach new goals by changed behavior is especially common in peer group situations and thus something that children have to deal with constantly.

## Yourself

You are, by far, the most likely source of negativity relative to goals you set. You know exactly how to undermine yourself. You know just what rationalizations to use for supporting a decision to abandon efforts at change. Justification for quitting is always close at hand; you can easily become your own worst enemy.

Obviously, the best way around the danger you present

yourself is to ensure that your goal payoff is achievable and worth the effort you put into realizing it. You also want to remain alert to the consequence of giving up on it.

Pursuit of a goal may require giving up other things temporarily. But do not become so goal-obsessed that you exclude other important dimensions of life. Your aim should be personal growth, not change just for the sake of change.

Assess where you want to realize change and pursue change with a clear awareness of the improvement you're aiming at. Setting specific goals with a realistic sense of the value payoff you anticipate will safeguard you here.

# 4

# Look Beyond the Obvious
# —Alternatives

In order to realize goals, you have to take action. There has to be at least one thing you can do to implement change. That much is undoubtedly obvious to you.

The question may then appear to be simply how to identify a way of making a change. Once you've done that, you're set, aren't you? Then it becomes a matter of just following through. Sometimes you'll have to cast around a bit for exactly what to do in a given situation; sometimes what to do is self-evident, and it only takes doing it to accomplish your goal.

No. Right there you have an illustration of the kind of thinking that as often keeps goals out of reach as results in positive steps to achieve them.

Why? Because it demonstrates a very limiting approach to implementing change. Identifying only one or two possible courses of action—and generally those that appear obvious—subjects you to a greater likelihood of being blocked. It takes only an impediment or two to thwart efforts at change, and often there are obvious impediments complicating follow-through on obvious courses of action. That commonly leads to copping out, taking no action because it's seen as too difficult or futile to carry out.

Let's imagine a common family situation. Adam is doing

poorly in school, and one of the main reasons for this is his failure to complete homework assignments. You want to see him do better. So you set as a specific goal ensuring that he do his homework every night without fail. To you that obviously means playing something of a truant officer, making him sit down with his homework and keeping him at it until it's done.

And then you think about what's bound to happen as a result of your acting as truant officer: You set yourself in the position of being the bad guy as far as Adam's concerned. You have to continually force him to do something he clearly hates doing. It's going to be one long series of orders and threats throughout the school year. Not only is that unlikely to appeal to Adam; it doesn't appeal to you either. And with that thought, there goes the chance for any program of change aimed at achieving the goal you'd set in this situation.

The difficulty here is that you've done little if anything to develop other approaches to reaching your goal. This is a general problem in implementing change. A perceived lack of alternatives is the single greatest obstacle in the way of attaining what is best for yourself and others.

A second common fault, also evident in the example above, is the tendency to judge the new alternative in isolation. You consider the implications of a truant officer's approach to your son's delinquency in the area of homework and shy away from taking action because of those. What you don't think to do is to compare the implications there with the consequences of doing nothing. Until you've made that comparison, you have no good basis for accepting or rejecting whatever course of action is under consideration.

To make a truly valid comparison, you must look beyond the present. Assess a possible course of action over the short and long term. Focusing on immediate considerations will frequently create a blindness to the real benefits or deficits in what you eventually decide to do.

So what should you do in this situation? Well, to begin with, you should put effort into developing as wide a range of action options as you can. Do that when first you see that a problem exists or when it first occurs to you there may be an opportunity to work a situation more to your advantage. Take the attitude that things have to change—they can't go on as they have up to now. People often shy away from change because they fear it will require uncomfortable adjustments. But then circumstances wind up controlling you. Finally Adam flunks out or fails to qualify for a program that would provide him greater opportunities for achievement. And then you have little if any time to develop and pursue options in the way of remedy.

With important decisions, pursue alternatives from a position of strength whenever possible, before the situation gets to a point where your options are severely limited. This means developing an action orientation to keep you continually abreast of possibilities and to keep sight of the positives and negatives implicit in what you're doing now.

Do this for yourself now: Think of a situation facing you that you'd like to change. On a piece of paper write down all of the things you could or might like to do (even if some of those seem unrealistic at first glance). To get beyond the limitations of your own perspective, ask others what they might do. When it comes to problems with children, it's surprising how often the children themselves can lead you to new alternatives. As you develop your list, keep in mind that you are operating in the here and now. You must consider current resources, obligations, and other factors that affect your ability to act. It may help you to write these down separately.

To give you an idea of how to develop your list, let's use the example of getting Adam to do his homework. We'll set up a two-column format, listing action possibilities on one side and resource considerations (including limitations) on the other.

The list of possible action alternatives isn't necessarily complete here, nor is the resources and limitations list. However, you can see what's involved in going beyond that first obvious choice, supervising Adam nightly in some kind of truant officer capacity.

| Action Possibilities | Resources and Limitations |
|---|---|
| Supervise Adam's doing his homework every night | Adam's ability—you know he can do better when he applies himself |
| Punish Adam for substandard performance in school | Adam's motivation—to him homework is the ultimate bore |
| Reward Adam for improved performance in school | Money—you can't afford special tutoring assistance |
| Get someone else to help Adam with his homework | Friends—Adam's two best friends are above-average students |
| Get Adam into a curriculum he enjoys more | Curriculum—there's only one basic fifth-grade program for everyone |
| Try to build an element of fun into Adam's homework | The time you have—limited |
| Talk to Adam's teachers about easing up on him | Adam's teachers—can't give him special attention he may require |

Note that once you've developed your list of possibilities, it's not always a matter of selecting just one of those on the list. If more than one proves attractive, there may be a way to combine them into a new or more specific alternative. Say the most appealing alternative above is building an element of fun into Adam's homework. But then you find yourself thinking it would be good to get someone to help him. Hey! Suppose you worked out an arrangement for Adam to work on homework assignments with his friends?

No doubt you can think of immediate objections to that. Of course, but then you can usually think of an objection to any line of action proposed. That's typically how resistance to change manifests itself. There's this immediate fear that the option favored won't work. Because it's a new course of action, you don't have any reassurance from past experience to rely on.

But experience is totally past-oriented. If you rely only on the experiences of the past, you're taking an approach to the future that largely rules out change. You're putting your goal beyond reach. You can't get somewhere different by following only the roads already traveled.

## KEEPING ALTERNATIVES MANAGEABLE

While it's important you develop a range of alternatives that goes beyond the obvious, there will be situations that do not require your exploring every option that may be possible. For one thing, simple practicality has to be considered. You could conceivably spend so much time developing alternatives that you don't get around to action that is called for. Besides that, once you start developing your list, that can grow to such length that you find the task of sorting out all the possibilities unmanageable.

Fortunately, several shortcuts can save you a lot of work in this area.

### *Settle for Something Merely Satisfactory*

Identify an option that provides a course you know will be okay, even if it might not be the best of all possibilities. This is a handy method for approaching situations that do not imply serious consequences.

For example, you are out with your daughter, Michelle, shopping for an item of clothing for school wear. You already know something about what you want—it has to be acceptable in terms of the school dress code and your own sense of what is appropriate for school. You'd like it to meet with Michelle's approval. She's going to be the one to wear it.

You and Michelle together identify a number of possibilities that meet needs in the areas of price, style, quality, and color. Once you've done that, you go to a store you have confidence in and buy the clothing article that meets the criteria you have set. You may do a little comparison shopping, but you're not going to run around for the entire day looking for the best of all possible buys just because there might be something better somewhere out there in another store. You simply want something that will do. The decision is not important enough for the two of you to spend a lot of time coming up with what might be judged the very best of available choices.

## Use a Process of Elimination

Identify the things you want an alternative to satisfy. List these in their order of importance. Then as soon as you hit on an option that meets the demands on your list, settle on that.

There are a couple of drawbacks to this shortcut. For one thing, while all the necessary demands may be accommodated, they may not be accommodated to the same degree in terms of the overall quality you desire.

Then too, you may not find an alternative that will accommodate all of the demands on your list. However, if that proves the case, you can either revise your list or settle for whichever option comes closest.

## Apply Some Kind of Simple Rule for Selection

You might opt for a rule of acceptability to the majority of those involved, if it's a question of something to satisfy several people. For example, in choosing a family vacation, rather than searching for an activity/destination that pleases everyone, you might decide to settle on one that just has majority support. Mom and Dad and Freddy want to go to the beach; Cindy wants to go somewhere where there's horseback riding. The family goes to the beach.

Or you might attach certain predetermined weights to the outcomes under each alternative and then go with the one that provides the highest total score with respect to outcomes. For example, in choosing where you send four-year-old Christopher to nursery school, you might be taking these factors into account, weighting them as indicated on a scale from 1 to 5.

- Christopher will be under the supervision of trained personnel with experience in preschool programs for children. (5)

- Christopher will/will not be exposed to religious instruction. (2)
- Christopher will be in a peer group you can reasonably expect will go to the same public/private school in later years. (2)
- Christopher will be in facilities that are clean, well heated, and well protected against any threat of fire. (5)
- Christopher will be kept under supervision until as late as 7:00 P.M. in the event parents are delayed on pickup after work. (5)
- You or your spouse will not have to go out of the way to drop off/pick up Christopher on the way to/from work. (3)
- Preschool training will give Christopher a head start in elementary reading and arithmetic skills. (4)

The list could run longer, but the point should be clear. You set a value on the various outcomes, making up your own scale. Then in examining alternatives, you go with which of the choices provides you the highest total score. If one of the outcomes is absolutely essential, then you can star that as requisite in any situation and combine the process of elimination with this scoring technique.

You can set your own rules for most any situation, but be alert to two possible problems.

First, *don't set rules in such a fashion that you automatically exclude options that are new or creative.* It's very easy to fall into setting rules that inevitably leave you with the same old options, and that's self-defeating.

Second, *keep in mind that rules that occur to you won't always make sense in a new situation.* When you're on unfamiliar territory, trying to locate an old landmark to go by can prove inappropriate for deciding on what direction to follow next.

Managing alternatives with shortcuts is necessary at times. But when it comes to important life decisions, there's no good substitute for knowing where all the possibilities lie. Think beyond the obvious. And keep track of the considerations that attach to each possibility.

A helpful way of keeping track of alternatives is to develop a chart that provides you a summary overview of all of them together, which makes comparisons much simpler. This is how such a chart might be organized.

| Alternative | Outcomes | Risk | Desirability | Cost |
|---|---|---|---|---|
| 1. | _____ | _____ | _____ | _____ |
|  | _____ | _____ | _____ | _____ |
|  | _____ | _____ | _____ | _____ |
| 2. | _____ | _____ | _____ | _____ |
|  | _____ | _____ | _____ | _____ |
|  | _____ | _____ | _____ | _____ |

*(Use a separate sheet for additional alternatives.)*

In the end, success or failure when it comes to identifying the best alternative will stem from your care to develop an adequate field of options. That means doing what you can to go beyond the obvious; it means forcing yourself into the consideration of possibilities that might at first seem impractical or uncomfortable for you.

Nothing is more detrimental to the total decision process than not doing a good job identifying possible alternatives and their outcomes before making a choice. (We'll discuss gaining insight into what's involved in the link between alternatives and outcomes in the next two chapters.) You may find it impossible to cover the whole range of possibilities before you have to act. However, be sure you don't opt for a shortcut too soon, lest you cut yourself off from the possibility of discovering what really would work best for you under the circumstances.

# 5

# Find Out What You Need
# to Know—Information

Information enables you to reduce the unknown to the known, both as far as facts are concerned and as far as feelings are involved. It helps you predict how likely and desirable the outcome of any action may be. That reduces your chance of making a mistake about the risks attached to any course of action you decide on. However, information does not by itself reduce risk, and it's very important you remember that when considering what to do in a given set of circumstances.

You obtain information in a number of ways:

- Through talking with other people
- By directly observing situations yourself
- Through reading others' reports
- By gaining relevant experience
- Through self-examination

When you get to specifics, that means a tremendous range of sources to refer to—a diversity of people, observations, reports, experiences, and feelings and motives of your own to take into account.

What are the information sources you customarily turn to when trying to decide on a line of action? Draw up a list for yourself. In particular, whom or what do you take into account when it comes to family situations? How do these fit into the categories of available sources? Are you taking advantage of as wide a variety of sources as is available to you?

You may not be able to or need to deal with every available information source in a given situation, but you should have a clear sense of what is available, in terms of both types of sources and specific sources. When it comes to making decisions, you want to be sure you haven't overlooked information sources that could help you get things into clear perspective.

You may not always need to interrogate other people, arrange on-the-scene observation of a situation you're concerned with, or read all that has been published about a relevant topic. But there is one information source you will have to turn to every time—*you*. Your priorities are always a relevant consideration in everything you choose to do. You want the decision you make to satisfy you, to reflect your value orientation and meet the goals you've set yourself. So thorough self-examination is always vital.

### HOW MUCH INFORMATION DO YOU NEED?

You need only enough information to make a sound choice among alternatives available. How much that is depends on you—what your priorities are in the areas of values and goals, and what determines that any risk involved is worth taking.

Because information collection requires an investment in time and effort, some people do a less than adequate job in this area. They don't look to all the available sources for input that could affect their view of possibilities. They may not look into what's involved in one or more of the alternatives available. They don't provide themselves the reassurance they could that the decision they make adequately meets their priorities and expectations.

Suppose the local elementary school is organizing a school band. Parents are advised that limited funds make it impossible for the school to provide the students instruments, but rental arrangements have been worked out for those without instruments of their own who wish to join the band. The Petersons, a family of modest means, are very concerned their daughter have the benefit of every opportunity to develop her musical talents. The Bergers, also a family of modest means, don't see that their daughter has any particular musical ability and are not concerned about opportunities in that area. Their priority is seeing her concentrate on more academic pursuits. Both girls have expressed only passing interest in joining the band.

Here you can see that the information needs vary for ensuring a choice that best reflects established priorities, even though it appears to be the same decision for both families. The Bergers likely feel they can decide "no" simply on the basis of knowing the rental fee is an expense they don't want to incur, since their daughter isn't that enthusiastic anyway. The Petersons would prefer not to incur a rental fee, but they do want their daughter to be part of the band. Their information need is clearly greater than that of the Bergers. Were they to come to a "no" decision eventually only on the basis of the information the Bergers considered, it would be clear the Petersons hadn't served their own priorities well. The Bergers wouldn't have that problem.

The example is on something of a simplistic level, but you can see the principle involved.

When it comes to decisions of greater complexity and import, it usually takes consideration of a wide variety of factors to be sure of understanding all possibilities for action. You'd think the problem of insufficient research would be the main problem here, given that information needs are so diverse and require an investment in time and effort. It is a common problem, but it's just as often the case that people collect too much information. Some people spend so much time collecting information that they never get around to making a decision.

While all important decisions typically require time so they receive the attention they should have, time can work against you when it comes to processing information. The more time you spend looking, the more probable it is that your information will become irrelevant or less accurate. The person you met five years ago who is still collecting information about the same critical decision is probably never going to decide. Information for this person has become a convenient cop-out, an excuse for inaction while giving the appearance of preparing for action.

If you're one of those who's continually gathering information for a decision you've yet to face up to, run a little test on yourself. Try to identify the one piece of information that would get you moving. Is it information that is available? If so, how come you haven't already collected it? Or is it information that you will never be able to get—for example, something that would guarantee the certainty of a desired result? You'll never dig up an iron-clad guarantee that things will go exactly as you want them to. You might as well spend your time doing something else.

To control any tendency to get hung up on information-gathering, set time limits on your research tasks. Then use that time constructively. Tell yourself, "By next week I'll have this information," "Within two weeks I'll have talked to these people and read this material," etc. Time checks are good reminders that you are serious about what you're doing. They're also useful for getting a handle on how long it may be before you think you can be in a position to make a decision.

### INFORMATION-GATHERING GUIDELINES

Gathering information can be an arduous task. One thing you certainly want to avoid is working hard and then coming up empty-handed. You want your information search to be as fruitful as possible. The following guidelines will help you:

*Begin by looking for information that would make you feel comfortable and ready to take action.* Work out a "need to know" list that will enable you to plan how you will go about getting information, where you will go for it, and why and when it will help you select a course of action. The unskilled decisionmaker tends to get into trouble by collecting information without knowing how or why it is going to help. Don't start amassing information until you know what you want.

*Consider the sources you're referring to.* Why are you using these instead of others? What possible biases do your sources have or reflect that might color the information provided? Are you referring to any sources on the recommendation of others? If so, what biases might the referring person have that relate to the area of your decision?

*Know your own biases.* Are you investigating with an open mind, or are you trying to confirm preset conclusions? Can you honestly say, "I've given equal consideration to other points of view"?

*Seek information you don't want to hear.* You know what you want to hear. Are you testing that with sources that will play devil's advocate with you? You must be alert even to possibilities you'd rather not acknowledge if you are to have a total view of the risks in any decision.

*Know the limitations of experts.* Everybody has a blind spot or two, and this includes the experts. Are you automatically deferring to expertise? Don't be too quick to defer. Remember, you, not the expert, are the one who has to live with the decision made.

*Recognize the shortcomings of experience.* Experience has its limits and should not be considered special, infallible information. Subject it to the same test of relevance and reliability as you do other information. Always keep in mind that rating an experience as good or bad is a very subjective determination. Don't jump to that subjective conclusion without first regarding the facts of the situation involved.

*Consider feelings as well as facts.* Objective data is important, but emotions and feelings can prove valuable as well. Take them into account with an eye to how they do or may influence things. For example, in talking with people, what do you hear with regard to their feelings on alternatives under discussion? Are those likely to be your feelings, too?

*Review the order in which you gather information.* Has one piece of information prematurely turned you away from other information possibilities? What would happen if you reversed the order? Would you have consulted a source you're now ignoring?

Yes, all this does seem a lot to take into account. However, once you get into the habit of opening yourself to new possibilities, you'll find yourself automatically more aware of the diversity of information sources you can turn to.

As for the guidelines, note that openness is a thread that runs through those, too. Coming to grips with your information needs is as much a question of attitude as of procedure. Prompt yourself into an open consideration of possibilities all along the line, and you'll find yourself automatically observing rules of thumb given here that at first you might think require memorizing one by one.

### MANAGING INFORMATION COLLECTED

When it comes to managing all the information there is to gather, you do have to organize yourself. You can collect considerable data and, unless you take an organized approach, find yourself swamped in a mass of detail. You won't know what to do, because you won't know how to go about drawing conclusions from what you have.

I've found it helpful to chart information in capsule form. That involves listing the sources of to-the-point information (research will always uncover some information that is beside the point), identifying the most relevant input from those

## Capsulizing Information*

Alternative being considered: _____

| The Best Sources | Best Information from Each Source | General Picture (Positive, Negative, Neutral) |
|---|---|---|

People spoken to:

| _____ | _____ | _____ |
| _____ | _____ | _____ |
| _____ | _____ | _____ |

Direct observations (including visits):

| _____ | _____ | _____ |
| _____ | _____ | _____ |
| _____ | _____ | _____ |

Readings:

| _____ | _____ | _____ |
| _____ | _____ | _____ |
| _____ | _____ | _____ |

Experiences:

| _____ | _____ | _____ |
| _____ | _____ | _____ |
| _____ | _____ | _____ |

Reflections (self-examination):

| _____ | _____ | _____ |
| _____ | _____ | _____ |
| _____ | _____ | _____ |

Overall rating
(+ 0 −): _____

*Although the number of lines given here under each category is the same, you will very likely find your entries vary in number according to category.

sources, and then stepping back for an overall impression on whether information obtained favors an alternative under consideration. The following chart shows how that can be done with each alternative. Once you've capsulized the applicable information in each case, it becomes a fairly simple matter of comparison to see how the alternatives stack up against each other.

As well as providing you an easy reference for comparisons, this sort of chart provides an excellent summary of steps taken to gather information. You can see at a glance which sources you've turned to and which you've overlooked or slighted. Sources won't always be conspicuous by their absence, mind you, but an alert eye will see a pattern to the omissions. However, when working to remedy omissions, keep to a realistic time frame. You don't want to fall into an endless search for every possible opinion and detail on the subject. You'll never be able to eliminate all the unknowns.

One important point bears emphasis: *The best-organized information search in the world won't help you reach the best decision if you haven't made sure to take into account all the alternatives you might develop.*

Don't get lost in a search for information before you've done what you can to see the options that are available. And in following through with the information-gathering step, recognize that new alternatives may still spring up for consideration. When they do, don't try to push them aside. Add them to the list of alternatives you previously identified.

# 6

# Predict and Evaluate Outcomes
—Consequences

Accurately predicting and judiciously weighing possible consequences (outcomes) is the best insurance for selecting a course of action that gets you what you want. In gathering information you are actually already working out your prediction of consequences. You are already putting yourself in a position to choose among them. In this step of the decision-making process, you compare alternatives according to the results each can or may lead to.

There are both good (positive) and bad (negative) consequences. Virtually any alternative you consider has some potential in both directions.

Any action you take has something of a ripple effect. There isn't just one consequence; there's a flow of consequences—opportunities opening up and closing at the same time or in some kind of succession. While there may be a particular consequence you are focusing on, there are always others to take into account. Choosing one doesn't rule out everything else, although it always rules out something. Moving toward a positive does not mean that you have no negative to contend with.

Consequences also occur along a time continuum. That's inherent in the ripple effect. Some will come about immediately or in an easily foreseeable short term. Others will develop over the long term. And that's true for both good and bad consequences.

Because long-term consequences may prove to be the most important, it is vital always to look beyond the present when considering a course of action. The failure to look beyond the present has severe implications, and it is so easy to fall for an immediate desired outcome without thinking of the difficulty that may later attach to the choice that's been made. To cite but one example, this is what so often happens when teenagers experiment with sex.

There's something of a countervailing precaution to take as well. Sometimes people focus so strongly on long-term benefits that they fail to take intermediate reality into account. A student chooses a difficult course of study in order to qualify for a particular college program, failing to realize it may be impossible to keep up with these studies. An ambitious worker takes on a special assignment in order to be in line for an eventual promotion, not thinking that it will require putting in impossibly grueling hours to complete and keep up with regular responsibilities.

Failure to take the short term into account can also keep hoped-for long-range consequences out of reach.

Predicting consequences is a matter of viewing information gathered with an eye to the results of any action contemplated. If you've been thorough in gathering information, you should be alert to possible outcomes for each alternative. You should have a sense of the likelihood that one or other outcome or series of outcomes will occur. However, since it's natural to have blind spots when it comes to predicting consequences, positive and negative, short term and long term, it's almost always helpful to share your predictions with others. Getting additional input expands your vision. It helps you eliminate biases and correct omissions where these skew your perspective on what can or may happen.

## WEIGHING CONSEQUENCES

Once you're reasonably sure you've looked at all the possibilities that exist for taking action and at the consequences likely in each case, you're ready to begin the process of elimination that leads to the action you will ultimately take. You eliminate alternatives you've identified by weighing the consequences in each against each other.

Weighing consequences is a matter of balancing two factors: *risk* and *desirability*—what is likely to happen in any case and what is important to you. Being realistic requires that you consider both the short term and the long term, recognizing that some trade-off may be necessary or advisable to ensure your getting what you most want.

The skilled decisionmaker works to arrive at the combination of risk and desirability that provides the best value. That means providing oneself the most favorable odds for gaining benefit out of the choices made.

There are three common patterns that people follow when it comes to striking a balance between risk and desirability.

### *The Dream Return*

The decider concentrates just on what is most desirable, pushing for that without considering risks seriously and without making adjustments that would improve chances of winning at least some advantage in the event the dream proves elusive. This pattern is typical of idealists who imagine perfect solutions can be or have been found to solve personal and/or social problems. It's typical of people who feel they have nothing to lose and everything to gain by going all out for what they most want.

### Catastrophe Avoidance

This approach to consequences emphasizes reducing the risk that something particularly undesirable may come about. Desirability enters into the picture in a backward sort of way, taken into account only through identifying what is least wanted. The choice of an action is made according to what seems most certain to eliminate the danger of that happening. Whatever movement the individual initiates is primarily a matter of backing away from something, not of moving toward a goal chosen for its desirable qualities.

You see this approach in operation when youngsters give in to peer pressures to do something they're not comfortable with rather than allow themselves to be thought up-tight or square. You see it when someone enters marriage in order to avoid winding up an old maid or arousing suspicions about "queer" sexual preferences.

### The Good Chance

The decider pays a lot of attention to the likelihood that a result that is at least somewhat desirable will be attained. There's a willingness to trade off certain desirables in exchange for a better chance of something adequate happening. There's a readiness to accept some risk in order to have a chance at getting something wanted, as opposed to focusing just on what is to be avoided at any cost.

Overall, the good chance pattern provides the best consistent results. The others can lead to good results—surprisingly good ones on occasion—but the law of averages works against them. Dream returns more usually fail to materialize, with the decider subsequently caught up in a morass of unwanted consequences he or she is unprepared for. Backing away from the threat of a catastrophe, usually subjectively defined, regularly leads to other difficulties and dissatisfaction. Opportunities are not recognized or assessed in terms of their positive potential, so that potential is rarely achieved.

Balancing risk and desirability requires the skillful use of information. Risk, for example, may be real or only seen as real by the person considering an action. The reality of risk is determined by collecting information to indicate a probability that something will or will not happen. But a lot of people don't take the time to assemble related facts systematically. They consider risk in terms of a hunch or in terms of limited past experience. While they respond to their conclusions as if the risk they see is real, they may be way off when it comes to predicting probabilities. Of course, some uncertainty always remains, but there is usually a good deal of information available on what may or can happen in choosing an alternative under consideration. Taking the time to ferret that out puts you on more solid ground when considering trade-offs aimed at keeping risk within acceptable bounds.

Desirability is determined through self-examination. You determine what is preferable by your answers to two questions: (1) What is important to me overall, and (2) What do I want in this specific instance? Here again it's important you be thorough in considering the issues. You can get into difficulty concentrating on what you want in a specific instance without taking into account what is important to you overall. It's that kind of half focus in the area of desirability that so often leads to choices for short-term benefit at long-term costs.

### MANAGING CONSEQUENCES

There is always a chance that the unpredictable will happen. Sometimes the results of a decision are better than anticipated (and that can happen even with decisions that are not well thought out). Sometimes they are worse (and that can happen even with well-considered decisions). The odds are in your favor if you follow a good chance pattern in reaching decisions. But there's no way you can predict everything with absolute certainty, even applying the best techniques.

You can probably take the unexpected bonuses in stride. It's likely you're more concerned with the difficulties unexpected problems might pose. Or, observing that some risk attaches to a decision, you may be scared away from an action because you don't think you could handle a difficulty you already see as possible. But then what of the benefit? And what of the consequences of doing nothing? Don't forget they may also include problems you'd just as soon avoid.

You can't eliminate risk, not even if you take a catastrophe avoidance approach to decisionmaking. You have to face up to the possibility that you may land a negative consequence in the process of reaching for a positive one. Of course that's disconcerting. But you needn't freeze with anxiety. You will still have the capability of managing consequences.

Simply in predicting consequences you've taken a major step toward managing them. You've eliminated the element of surprise. You can plan for contingencies.

You predict a consequence. Then you assess it in terms of whether or not it is worth the risk involved in reaching for it. Finally, you make a judgment with regard to the total cost involved—can you make a commitment of your resources (time and energy, as well as material) to keep on top of things that happen, good or bad? That's the management question.

Managing is knowing what you will have to do when something occurs. It requires a view of the total picture—how the consequences will affect you directly, how they will affect others around you, how they will affect the setting in which you live. You have to take each of these related points into account in order to manage things to your general benefit. Taking them into account requires answering these key questions:

- Can you afford this consequence in terms of time, energy, and other resources available to you?

- What specific fallout might this outcome have with regard to the people and the world around you?
- Do you have some specific plan or suggestions in mind for helping others to deal with the fallout from your decision?
- Do you have a contingency plan in the event things go wrong?
- What's the worst possible thing that could go wrong? Could you manage that?
- Are you prepared for success? If things turn out as desired, what future action might be required or expected of you?

Ask yourself these questions once you've identified the action alternative that most appeals to you after weighing the consequences attached to each alternative. If you find that you can manage the consequences, even should things not turn out as you'd like, then you're ready for the next step: action.

# 7

# Follow Through on Your Decision —Action and Review

You've sorted things out systematically. Now it's time to move. Make your decision. Follow through on the choice you've identified and do what needs doing to set the wheels of change in motion.

### RESPONSIBLE ACTION

Whatever your decision, how you've come to it implies a conscious acceptance of responsibility. You've considered the positive and negative consequences and made your own selection of which to reach for and which to risk. You can't blame someone else for whatever happens as a result of your choice. But then, the credit doesn't go to someone else either.

How often do you hear people excuse themselves for winding up in an unexpected, difficult-to-manage situation with remarks like "Nobody told me this would happen," "It seemed okay because everyone else was doing it," or "I don't see why people have to follow these silly rules, anyway?" These statements all cry out the same message: I did something and now I don't want to have to deal with the consequences.

But whether you want to or not, you do have to deal with the consequences. So the best approach is to take them into account as much as possible beforehand. You can't really avoid the responsibility for what you do, even though you may try to duck it. The consequences remain. However, if you've taken those into account and prepared yourself for them, you're not likely to be taken completely by surprise by them. The action you choose is by definition responsible because you've already recognized yourself as the agent for whatever change is brought about as a result of it.

At this point, the only guideline is to follow through with the action chosen. The only caution is not to introduce some element of variation in that action that could also introduce a consequence you haven't fully taken into account.

### REVIEWING THE ACTION TAKEN

In addition to accepting accountability for what you do, responsibility means being responsive to the results. You've taken an initiative in bringing about change. That's not just an isolated, one-time act; it's a continuing process. It's somewhat like driving a car. You start it and point it in the direction you want to go, but that's not all you have to do. In order to get where you want to be, you have to keep a hand on the steering wheel and a foot ready at both the accelerator and the brake.

All too often the so-called decisive person is marked by an unwillingness to be responsive. The attitude is, "I made this decision and I intend to stick with it as made." Now, it's nice to be this assertive when it comes to taking action, but it's not a good approach to hold to all of the time.

Because decisions and their outcomes evolve in the future, new variables constantly enter the picture. You have to steer through or around those. You have to take stock of what you're doing and where you are so that you can identify and adjust to new developments that might otherwise throw you off track. That means (1) assessing the impact of the decision upon yourself and others, in particular through getting feedback from those directly involved; (2) examining the decision process as results unfold so that omissions can be identified and corrected in related future actions; and (3) communicating how the decision was made and how it is progressing as it makes its way into the future.

In short, simply making a decision and implementing it is not enough. How it is put into action and experienced along the way by both the decisionmaker and others who may be affected also figures into the overall assessment of quality in the choice made.

Making a choice is not a stop-and-go activity. It's a dynamic process. There's always the opportunity to make changes and adjustments along the way, to accommodate what you learn in the meantime. It's a process that permits mistakes because mistakes can be corrected. Finally, it's a process that embodies a sensitivity to the needs, attitudes, and priorities of others, because these affect you in your relationship to the world around you. Depending upon who you are and where you live, there are certain limitations and resources and attitudes that must be considered as you review possible courses of action. You do have to acknowledge that you are not complete unto yourself; you are part of a larger whole—of a family, of a community, of society at large.

## RATIONAL VS. EMOTIONAL DECISIONS

The seven-step process set out in this section is a rational approach to taking action. However, it does not exclude whatever feelings or emotions may play a part in reaching a decision.

Feelings and so-called intuitive responses ("gut" reactions) are important considerations in any decision. You can't always put a finger on all of the reasons you have for doing certain things or for feeling good about what you do.

What you can do is learn to be more in tune with your feelings. That means recognizing what they are and when they come into play. You can usually do a lot more to get at what's behind a feeling or intuitive reaction than you do. Often a feeling about something has roots in an information or experience base that you can't easily pinpoint. However, you can usually clarify what lies behind a feeling by making an effort to explain what it is and sharing it with those around you. The crucial thing here is to *go as far as you can to identify why you feel a certain way about things.* What memories come up? What expectations do you feel and where do they have their origin? Of course, you will find that some things cannot be explained completely, but the effort to understand should always be made.

The distinction between rational and emotional decisions is not that the former takes only facts into consideration while the latter goes according to feelings. The rational decision takes facts *and* feelings into consideration. It represents an awareness of the reality outside of you; it takes into account the preferences you've developed in your own experience of life. An emotional decision tends to ignore outside reality and, in so doing, fails to take into account the consequences that reality introduces.

Making good decisions requires effort. It takes more than merely understanding how a good decision is made. It also means a real commitment on your part to examine your skills honestly and do what you have to in order to improve them.

You've picked up this book out of a concern to provide your child guidance. The brief course provided you here in Part One gives you a framework within which to do that. Making it your personal framework is a major step in qualifying yourself for the task ahead.

# PART II

# *Your Family Situation and Home Environment*

---

The material here applies to you and your family regardless of the age of your child(ren). Use this section as a resource guide to refer to in implementing general policies and in responding to situations encountered at different age levels.

# 8

# Knowing Yourself and
# Your Family Situation

It's tempting to announce that you should delay trying to teach your child to make decisions until you're sure you're doing it absolutely right yourself. Certainly that would be ideal. But that would also be overlooking one important reality. You're a parent now, and you have to provide your child guidance now. You can't leave him or her in limbo somewhere for a couple weeks or months while you develop new abilities.

To the degree you are still learning to make good decisions yourself, you may not be confident of your ability now to provide the kind of guidance you'd like. Take heart. As with any skill-building process, early attempts to put into practice all you've covered in Part One will at times prove discouraging, frustrating, and even terrifying. But consider this: You have to make decisions all along, anyway. Even though you may not have the immediate payoff of feeling in control, you will nevertheless be moving to control as you begin to take necessary considerations systematically into account. You'll already be taking a better approach than you were before. Your child will experience an immediate benefit in seeing you initiate change, in watching you assume a more positive control over the choices you have to make every day for both yourself and your family.

Your decisions and actions have a formative impact on your child, even those that are not directed primarily at him or her. Your first teaching task may well be to provide an example of how one introduces positive change into one's life. That means beginning with a realization of where you are now in terms of how you make decisions and how you encourage your child in the area of preparing to make decisions.

### YOU AS A DECISIONMAKER

Part One provides the information needed to determine whether you're taking into account what you ought to when making decisions. You can run a quick review check on yourself by going down this list of questions related to the seven-step process described there.

#### Decisionmaker's Inventory

*Values*

_____ Do you know what values are important to you and why?
_____ Do you know which are more important and why?

*Goals*

_____ Do you know how to identify specifically what you want out of a decision?
_____ Do you know why you want it?
_____ Do you know how to set up a program for getting it?

*Alternatives*

_____ Do you know how to develop possibilities for taking action to reach your goal?
_____ Do you know your resources and limitations when it comes to taking action?

*Information*

_____ Do you know what information sources to turn to and what kind of information to look for?
_____ Do you know how to manage the information you get?

*Consequences*

_____Do you know what consequences to anticipate?
_____Do you know how to weigh them against each other?
_____Do you know how to manage the consequences you get, whatever they might be?

*Action*

_____Are you prepared to take action?
_____Do you accept responsibility for what happens?

*Review*

_____Are you prepared for success?
_____Do you have an eye open for adjustments you may have to make either to keep things on course or to put them on a better course?

Consider your answers carefully. Don't be too glib with your responses. Think of an important decision you've faced recently or that you face now. Can you fill in the blanks that are implicit here: your values, a clearly stated goal, the possibilities for action to achieve that, etc.?

Use this inventory to develop an overview of your situation whenever you face decisions of importance. It will provide you both a quick-reference checklist of considerations that must be taken into account and an outline within which to organize decisionmaking activities.

### YOU AS A PARENT

Do your attitudes and actions as a parent contribute to your child's readiness to make his or her own decisions? Are you doing what you can to educate your child for independence?

Educating for independence yields specific positive results. In the Introduction we've already identified involvement, control, freedom, and a sense of doing something worthwhile as payoffs the child experiences for himself. Let's look also at the payoffs evident in your child's relations with the surrounding world. We can point to three in particular: respect, power, and responsibility.

### Respect

Respect is the readiness to take other people's needs and feelings into account as one pursues and explores his or her own. It grows out of an awareness that one's world meshes with others, that how one takes others into account influences the quality of one's own life.

Respect is directly linked to a sense of self-worth. It develops only in an atmosphere where the person is encouraged to express himself or herself and where there is a feeling that people care and are willing to listen to each other.

Parents who lack respect for themselves or each other will have a hard time teaching their children respect. Not until the parents gain self-esteem and learn to recognize worth in others is it likely that their child will make progress here. It is essential that parents show their child they think him or her worthy.

Your child's sense of worth is directly affected by your attitudes. Unless you do what you can to encourage feelings of self-worth and recognition of worth in others, your child is going to be difficult to work with. Feeling unworthy, he or she will see no advantage to involvement. He or she will not value his or her own input or ability to effect positive change. He or she will not recognize the potential for gain through cooperation with others and so will tend to be indifferent to others' needs and feelings.

### Power

Power is the ability to introduce change into one's world in a manageable fashion. Teaching your child to make decisions is another way of saying, "You can influence how things affect your life. You can take a hand in defining who and what you will be."

As a parent, the idea is to create an environment in which your child learns how to influence things to his or her own advantage. In the home, you can set up something of a laboratory in which your child, safeguarded under a watchful eye, learns the connection between action and consequences.

You can begin teaching your child about power as early as age three or four. By that time children begin to see what goes into taking an action and how consequences grow out of actions. You can provide opportunities for meaningful choices, developing situations wherein the child learns what it takes to get control. By giving weight to the child's place in the family, you show that his or her input has an impact on family decisions. By encouraging him or her to make certain decisions alone, you help your child understand how to use the available resources and what limitations to take into account.

### Responsibility

Responsibility is the willingness to be held accountable for your actions. You accept that the consequences resulting from an action are a product of your decision and not to be blamed on someone or something else. Responsibility involves a recognition that you are a part of human society. You acknowledge that your actions can have an impact on others, and you accept limitations aimed at protecting others from possible harm as a result of what you could do.

Encouraging responsibility in your child starts with demonstrating responsibility yourself. Children are very alert to adults' inconsistencies in this area. They are not apt to understand why they should curtail behaviors that adults routinely display. They rebel at being held accountable for actions and consequences that adults expect to get away with.

Teaching responsibility in family interactions is the first step to prompting responsible behavior in relations with the outside world. You're most likely to get positive results when guidelines for responsibility are established jointly by all family members and apply to all, even the youngest child in the family.

## *Rating Yourself*

The following questions will help you gauge your present performance as a parent when it comes to educating for independence. Each pinpoints an action or attitude that contributes to development of the quality indicated in your child's behavior.

Are you doing all you can to promote behavior in your child that reflects an attitude of respect, an awareness of power, and an acceptance of responsibility? A *no* answer to any of the questions below indicates an area for work and improvement. Occasional *no* answers indicate that the general pattern of your behavior as a parent is pretty good, but with room for improvement. A lot of *no* answers indicates a major need for reorientation of your parenting efforts.

### Parent's Self-Evaluation Inventory

*Respect:* As a parent do you

_____Create an openness that allows all family members to express their feelings?

_____Ask for your child's opinion to show you value what the child thinks or feels?

_____Establish regular periods for listening to and dealing with problems?

_____Explain why certain things are important to you, e.g., privacy and personal property, and extend respect in these areas to your child?

_____Openly acknowledge respectful behavior on the part of your child?

_____Allow all family members to have a say about how their time is being used?

_____Isolate your child when a reprimand is in order, so as not to humiliate him or her in front of others?

_____ Admit you don't have all the answers?

_____ Demonstrate that you can laugh at yourself and admit to your mistakes?

_____ Allow your child to participate in family decisions?

_____ Acknowledge the strengths you see your child display, even when you're pointing out a weakness?

_____ Encourage and promote listening so all members of the family have an "audience"?

_____ Show how you've taken others into account when making decisions that have an effect on them?

_____ Accept that your child will increasingly seek to establish value priorities of his or her own?

_____ Administer discipline with a care not to attack your child's sense of self-worth?

_____ Encourage helping relationships among all family members?

*Power:* As a parent do you

_____ Do things to promote independent action on the part of your child?

_____ Emphasize strengths and skills, including those not normally recognized in school or peer group situations?

_____ Allow your child to take occasional risks?

_____ Permit mistakes, knowing they are learning opportunities?

_____ Devise situations where your child can experience success?

_____ Help your child deal with rough spots in trying to carry out a decision, rather than step in and take over for him or her?

_____ Develop certain responsibilities for your child in the daily activities of family life?

_____ Show your child his or her input has an effect on family decisions?

_____ Make clear the kind of decisions your child is not ready to make and why?

_____ Establish readiness signs so that your child will know when he can expect to exercise more power?

_____ Pay attention to behavior-related difficulties so you can help your child find new ways of managing problem situations?

_____ Provide your child recognition for the successful completion of an action or task?

_____ Prepare your child for success in his or her endeavors so that he or she learns to maintain the positive momentum achieved as a result?

_____ Allow your child to experience resource limitations without stepping in immediately to relieve frustration there?

_____ Encourage flexibility in your child's pursuit of a course of action rather than insist on rigid follow-through of preset plans?

_____ Refrain from imposing solutions obvious to you when your child is trying to work through a problem?

*Responsibility:* As a parent do you

_____Make consequences clear when it comes to certain behavior or demonstrated lack of responsibility?

_____Point to consequences resulting from behavior as part of the choice your child makes when deciding on a course of action?

_____Ensure that rules for acceptable behavior are clearly stated and apply to all family members?

_____Display the same standard of behavior in interaction with others around you that you expect your child to display?

_____Avoid blaming others around you for difficulties that arise as a consequence of action you've taken?

_____Acknowledge inconsistencies in your own behavior as a matter for open discussion?

_____Allow your child to experience the negative consequences of an action without automatically stepping in to relieve him or her of the need to face up to them?

_____Encourage your child's participation in group activities as a way of developing greater social consciousness?

_____Give your child a voice in determining rules and rule changes within the family circle?

_____Create opportunities for the child to establish his or her own standards for responsible behavior?

_____Demonstrate a willingness to act in situations where the child cannot exert control and responsible behavior is actually discouraged or penalized?

## WHAT'S YOUR FAMILY ROUTINE?

Many parents fail to take into account how the normal day-to-day life of the home contributes to their child's growth toward independence. Family routines provide a rich set of opportunities for learning to make decisions. You don't always have to do something very different. Often it's simply a matter of using what you have going for you already.

One important consideration in reviewing family routines can too easily be overlooked: the effect of those routines on you. The tendency is to focus all the attention on how routines influence the child's learning new skills. Of course you have to emphasize that. But don't forget that you're part of the process, too. The home environment must encourage your efforts as well as your child's; otherwise you will find it inconvenient or burdensome to provide the necessary direction.

You also have to take into account how your family is affected by interaction with others. Your home isn't an island that no one leaves or comes to. Others step into the picture on a regular, maybe even daily basis. Who they are and how you and your child relate to them also affect the potential for learning here.

So take a few moments to look at family routines insofar as these determine how relationships develop in and around the home.

### The Things You Do as a Family

Activities as a complete family group are especially important for learning decisionmaking skills. They provide the best opportunity for sharing, for giving everyone a chance to contribute, and for gaining insight into each person's needs and feelings as a member of the family.

Three common events especially conducive to teaching decision skills are family recreational activities, the family meal(s), and the family meeting. Each provides a group setting, and each provides ways for people to learn about interacting with others.

*Family recreational activities.* Let's take as an example planning a family trip. This provides an excellent set of circumstances within which to apply the decisionmaking process and see it work. Each family member, including even children as young as three to four years of age, can easily imagine preferences he or she would like to see accommodated. Each member is likely to participate with enthusiasm in the choice of destination and/or activities once it's clear that input will be seriously considered.

You can organize planning a trip to follow the seven-step process for making good decisions. Your child benefits from the opportunity to follow each step with you through to a result that he or she has some voice in. You benefit from the same opportunity and from the chance to learn more about your child's values and preferences in this situation.

### The Family Trip Decision

| *The Decision Process* | *How Accommodated* |
| --- | --- |
| Define the situation and why it is important. | Parents explain the opportunity and what limits exist. Emphasis is on choosing a destination/ activities that everyone can enjoy. |
| Identify specific value and goal priorities. | What are the things we like to do? What would we like to get out of this trip? What are some of the differences in what we like? |
| Develop alternatives. | Look through travel folders. Consider personal destination preferences and suggestions from others. |
| Dig out and process information. | What are the advantages/features of each possibility—locale, weather, activities available, etc.? What feelings does each person have about these? |
| Consider risks and outcomes. | Discuss possible problems associated with each choice. Identify good and bad outcomes. Describe the impact of consequences that may attend each choice. |
| Take action. | Once a destination is selected, have each family member assume the responsibility for some task of preparation—making a list of clothes to bring, finding out more about activity schedules, putting things in order for the family's absence from home, etc. |
| Evaluate your decision. | As the trip unfolds, review what information you overlooked or misinterpreted, what unexpected outcomes you're experiencing, whether there is a general satisfaction with the trip. These things can be recorded so they will be remembered when the next trip decision comes up. |

You can apply this framework to virtually every decision you make as a family planning an activity together. Recreational activities are especially valuable learning experiences because it's generally easy to get children to participate actively. The process unfolds along lines even young children easily understand. You can actually express it in terms children naturally use themselves when it comes to deciding what to do. The tie-in may not be exact, but observe how closely the terms children use mirror what happens in the process outlined above.

- "What shall we do?"
- "What do you want to do?"
- "What can we do?"
- "What's the most fun?"
- "Yeah, but what happens if we do that?"
- "So okay, let's do that!"
- "I'm glad we did that."/"I wish we hadn't done that."

If part of your family routine does not include planning special events that involve everybody, you are missing one of the best opportunities for introducing your child easily to decisionmaking skills.

*Family meals.* Because of their regularity, family meals are especially good for involving your child in what goes into everyday decisions. It's customary in most families to discuss the events of the day over dinner, and that discussion commonly includes references to things planned, actions taken, and the results of actions taken.

You can help educate your child simply through the manner in which you discuss your decisions and their outcomes. You can encourage questions so that your child recognizes your decisions to be the result of a process, not just the product of arbitrary whim, which is what parental decisions too often seem to children.

You can also encourage your child to share his or her plans and experiences with the rest of the family. This will tend to prompt him or her into expressing something of why and how he or she acted or intends to act whatever the situation. With focused, process-related questions (as opposed to judgmental questions that have the effect of imposing your view without clarifying process), you can foster a sharper awareness in your child of how he or she can ensure the most favorable results from his or her actions.

The last few minutes of a meal are particularly suited to the airing of concerns or problems that involve the entire family or color the relationship between members of the family. Is there a problem with a sibling? Is there resentment about a rule that doesn't seem to make sense? These are important concerns for the child. Your attention to them provides another means of illustrating the link between actions and consequences and the fact of an impact beyond just the child alone.

*The family meeting.* Unfortunately, many families operate on a schedule that precludes much shared time together in special activities or even daily meals. That means less scope for interaction that could otherwise educate the child to a responsible appreciation of his or her place in the family group. Your child won't readily see how everyone counts when it comes to setting rules, choosing family goals, or dealing with problems that affect the entire family. He or she will feel less involved.

Where work or activity schedules are such that family times together are occasional at best, it is advisable to plan regular family meetings. You cannot realistically expect your child to identify with family values and goals if it is not clear to him or her that a cohesive family relationship exists. Regularly scheduled family meetings can do much to overcome whatever deficit exists in the time family members otherwise spend together as a group. You ensure your child a regular experience of the family functioning as a unit in which he or she plays a meaningful part. The benefit in terms of understanding family decisions and how they are reached will be substantial.

Even if you do spend routine time together as a family, sharing leisure activities and mealtimes, it can still be useful to plan regular family meetings. You can use these to discuss problems at some length, to establish family policy, to set family goals, and/or to define responsibilities for the various family members. Leisure activities and mealtimes do not always lend themselves to the more serious concerns that inevitably arise from time to time. (We'll discuss how to set up a family meeting at more length in Chapter 13.)

## Times Together with Part of the Family

The most frequent group experience in the family occurs when one parent is in contact with one or more children. This can be in the context of driving youngsters to after-school activities, helping with homework, watching television, bath time, or having lunch or a snack together.

These are important times because they provide for a special kind of interaction. Because they are frequently one-to-one situations, the child often finds it easier to open up, to share personal feelings without other siblings around. These are particularly good times to focus on the individual differences that exist among children. You have direct contact in which you can encourage, compliment, praise, and provide input into very personal problem areas.

You can become more aware of the interaction/intervention possibilities here by making a log of the kinds of things you do separately with one or several of your children on a daily basis. Once you realize what those are, you can plan to take advantage of them.

While we don't spend much time watching television in my family, my thirteen-year-old daughter has a favorite program that I watch together with her just about every week. I have found it an excellent opportunity for nonthreatening interaction that is a learning experience for both of us. We both focus on the program, and during commercial breaks we discuss what is going on and why. We try to establish what we might do in similar situations. Because of the nature of the program, we are able to examine the decision process of the characters and even discuss the different standards some of them follow in dealing with what is happening. In doing this, I try to get my daughter to give examples of people she knows like the ones on TV and to tell how she feels about them. I consistently find that through sharing this event communication opens up and discussions go on into other areas of concern.

The simplest event can be made into a meaningful exchange. Be alert to the opportunities you have every day to stimulate a broad perspective on even the routine experiences in your child's life.

### Times Together as a Parent

Although you might not have expected to consider this as part of the family routine affecting your child's education for independence, your privacy as a parent is very important. Whether you operate as a two-parent family or are a single parent, it is vital you have some uninterrupted time to yourself.

Several things can be done to promote this privacy. You can have an "off-limits" room that is your special place and out of bounds to the children. You can set a time before dinner to be by yourself or in the company of your spouse. Better yet, you can establish a weekly time to go out to dinner or share an event without the children.

This isn't selfish in any negative sense. It's recognizing a need that most people have—a time free of hassles, a time to review what's been happening with you or members of the family.

Parent-to-parent communication is essential. So many things relating to making decisions require consistent parent behavior, and this is made easier by advance discussion and planning. Simply being a provider is not enough to fulfill your child's needs for guidance. Your child needs help, and you are the best source for much of the help that is needed. The private time you share with your spouse allows you a moment to reestablish your own priorities. It provides you the opportunity for exchange with your partner to review those priorities and devise strategies that help ensure managing your child's problems effectively.

Preserving private time is particularly important as a means of showing your child that you have needs, too. It teaches him or her to respect your privacy. That is a basic requirement if your child is to learn to take the needs and feelings of others into account in what he or she decides to do.

### Time Your Children Have to Themselves

The core question in any decision is "what to do." That's the same question children have when it comes to free time.

Many young people do not have the foggiest notion about what to do with themselves. Consequently, the parent will often have to supply some alternative suggestions to support a child who is floundering in this area. Hobbies, reading, listening to music, writing letters, practicing a musical instrument, and working on athletic skills are just some of the possibilities for solo activity beneficial to the child. Each of these serves in some way to broaden his or her background of experience, to develop talents that will be useful or enjoyable throughout life.

Your child may not automatically turn to this kind of activity on his or her own. It may well be that you have to foster interests by making suggestions and even by initially requiring exposure to certain things. Years ago, beginning with the oldest of our four children, we required each child to read for thirty minutes every day. They could read what they liked, but they had to do it for thirty minutes. If they had no idea of what to read, we would provide the material. Eventually reading became an enjoyable habit for all our children, one they regularly opted for in their free time.

Time alone is also time for children to discharge the responsibilities they have been assigned. Those include tasks around the home and schoolwork. In each case, circumstances can contribute to your child regularly experiencing a sense of accomplishment, and the recognition you provide goes far toward reinforcing that.

A constructive use of free time commonly returns a high level of satisfaction, particularly if the parent is conscientious about recognizing efforts made and accomplishments won in this context. Free time use also gives parent and child additional insight into what the child values and why. It is an important part of promoting self-discipline in your child.

### *Time Your Child Spends with Other Children*

As your child moves from infancy through the preschool years, there will be increasing contact with other children. This contact may be formal (nursery school or play group) or informal (having a friend over, playing with other kids on the block). In either case, there is an interaction that either you or some other adult may be observing. These observations are important, because they give you valuable information about how your child relates in social situations.

As children increasingly participate in peer group activities, they begin to learn how their actions affect others; they become more aware of the impact others have on them. How the child relates to others and what he or she does or does not do in relating to others tells you a lot about his or her self-esteem, assertiveness, consideration of others, and understanding of individual differences.

Get feedback from your child on a regular basis as to his or her relations with peers. How does your child get along in class? Who are his or her friends? Is your child a loner in certain situations? What relationships does he or she enjoy and why? Teachers, babysitters, grandparents, other adults, and other children can provide you with valuable insights, too.

*Time You Spend with Other Parents*

This, too, may seem an unusual category to mention as contributing to your child's learning to make decisions. It's an often overlooked time that has excellent educational potential for parent and child alike.

Time spent with other parents is a natural for sharing ideas. This can happen informally, or you can set up a formal arrangement for exchanging information and viewpoints. The benefit to you is an increased flow of information about situations you're involved in with your child and that he or she faces outside the home. It becomes easier for you to establish consistent guidelines for monitoring your child's behavior and for expressing your own expectations in the area of behavior.

Parents have enough trouble dealing with children on their own. When other children exert pressures on your child, the potential for problems expands. And while you are trying to hold the line in teaching responsible behavior, it often seems other parents are indifferent to concerns on that score. But most parents do care. They probably feel as overwhelmed as you do at times. By exchanging information, you and they feel more confident of decisions made about family policies or resolving difficulties with children. You gain a broader perspective for guiding your child into responsible behavior.

Regular contact with other adults who have occasion to observe your child's actions and response to consequences is also helpful. Participation in parent-teacher meetings can be especially valuable, since outside of the family it is your child's teacher(s) more than anyone else who commonly sees his or her pattern of behavior and the sort of situations your child enters into in the course of deciding his or her own actions.

*Evaluating Your Family Routine*

Take some time to consider your family routines. Are things so organized that they contribute to the development of awareness and skills in your child? Are you providing yourself the opportunities you need to ensure you are effective in educating for independence? Does family routine contribute to your child's growth as a responsible individual, able to deal with the world around him and understanding and considerate of the needs and feelings of others?

In completing this evaluation, don't try to give "correct" answers. It's not a matter of grading your performance on a scale that runs from "good" to "bad." It's a matter of developing an awareness within yourself of what opportunities your family routine now provides you and what you can possibly do to increase those opportunities or use them to better advantage.

### Family-Routine Review

*Time spent together:*

_____How often does the family eat together?

_____Are meals made an opportunity for all members of the family to share experiences and discuss problems?

_____Is any day of the week set aside for a special family dinner?

_____How often does the family share leisure time together?

_____Do all members of the family have a chance to influence decisions on what activity to pursue?

_____Is there a family trip each year?

_____Are there regular family events that involve everyone?

_____Are there tasks around the home that the family all pitches in to work on?

_____Are special times scheduled for family meetings?

_____Do family members all see each other in the morning before school or work/in the evening after school or work?

_____Does the family attend religious services together regularly?

_____Is there a day when most family members do nothing?

*Your time spent alone with your child(ren):*

_____Which parent disciplines the child?

_____Who dresses the child?

_____Do children come home for lunch?

_____Do you drive or escort your child to or from outside activities?

_____Do you set aside a special time to be alone with your child?

_____Do you share a particular interest with your child?

_____Do you share particular tasks with your child?

_____ Do you assist your child in completion of homework assignments?
_____ Does your child feel free to discuss personal problems with you? Does he or she do so?

*Your time together with your spouse:*

_____ Do you schedule time together each week without the children?
_____ Do you have clear rules on private space and time to yourselves in the home?
_____ Do you use at least some of your time together to exchange viewpoints and set policies or plan activities affecting the children?

*Your child's time alone:*

_____ Does your child complain of having nothing to do?
_____ Does your child express interest in a particular hobby or leisure activity he or she can pursue alone?
_____ Does your child have assigned responsibilities to perform alone?
_____ Is there an area in the home that is "off limits" to others where your child can spend time alone, even if at other times that is shared space?
_____ Does your child have time alone to pursue his or her own interests?
_____ Do you express interest in your child's efforts and achievements when it comes to completing tasks or projects?
_____ Is it evident that your child generally spends time alone in goal-directed pursuits? Or does he or she passively let the world go by? Does he or she get into mischief?

*Your child's time with other children:*

_____ Does your child take part in after-school activities?
_____ Do your child's friends come over to play regularly?
_____ Does your child play on any teams?
_____ Does your child appear to be a follower or a leader?
_____ Does your child appear to be a loner?
_____ Does your child get into fights?
_____ Do you know who your child's friends are?
_____ How does your child spend time with the friends he or she has?

*Your time with other parents/adults:*

_____ Do your friends include parents facing concerns about their children that are similar to your concerns about your children?
_____ Do you share experiences and ideas about parenting?
_____ How often do you discuss parenting concerns with other adults?
_____ Do you use other adults as a regular information source when facing decisions that affect family members?

Look back to the preceding text for a sense of how to adjust elements of your family routine that you are not sure of or do not think contribute satisfactorily to your child's developing responsible behavior. Discuss your family routines with other family members, your child(ren) as well as your spouse. What do they see as areas for improvement? And equally important, what routines do they find provide them the structure and opportunity to practice good decision skills? Always keep in mind that it's as important to know what you're doing right as to know what you could do better.

### DO YOU KNOW YOUR CHILD?

In order to help your child, you've got to go beyond polishing your skills and adjusting your attitudes and family routines. Those are essential considerations, of course, but there's one more to take into account: your child's uniqueness as an individual. Helping your child make choices means being willing to accept the fact that he or she is unique and will approach and act upon things differently than you do.

Differences are okay. They are what give us individuality. The idea is to make them work to good effect.

For a parent, that's often not easy. It's hard for a parent not to expect to see his or her value priorities duplicated in the child. After all, it's not as if your child arrived equipped with a full set of his or her own. You've had to teach values and set goals until the child could understand them personally.

It seems so reasonable to expect a child would see things according to how parents train him or her to see things. But it isn't. The world looks different to your child. A child is smaller; other things loom bigger. A child is weaker; what is no threat to you frightens him or her. A child is inexperienced; things that frighten you have no meaning for him or her. A child is more recently on the scene; the world around offers strange fascinations. How could a child keep from drawing his or her own conclusions about things? A child has to in order to cope with the world as he or she experiences it.

With this in mind, let's take a look at the difference in how you see yourself and how your children see themselves. This is easily done through developing what I call the Real You Collage.

Fill in the details for yourself in each area indicated. What emerges is a composite picture, pieces that blend and fade into each other to form one image—you.

Then, assuming your child is able to understand the category descriptions given, have him or her fill in the details about him- or herself. Then compare the two profiles for similarities and differences. There will be more differences.

### The Real You Collage

*The Physical You*
The way you see yourself and the way others see you

*The Leisure You*
What you like to do in your free time

*The Accomplished You*
The things you're proud of achieving

*The Social You*
Whom you feel comfortable with

*The Situated You*
Where you exist and what you feel about it

*The Sad You*
What gets you down and what disappointments have affected your life

*The Happy You*
What pleases you and what satisfaction you've achieved in life

*The Guilty You*
What contradictions you experience in yourself and in your behavior toward others; where you think you go wrong

If one of your first reactions to seeing your child's profile is to say or think, "That's not right. Now, you know you . . . !" then it's a safe bet you have some difficulty accepting differences in your child. Otherwise your response would not be aimed at having things phrased the way you'd have expected to see them put.

In defining the "situated you," for example, you might very well indicate the country and city in which you live, the block your house or apartment is on, your living quarters, and your work environment, then sum up your feelings about each of those. Your child may have responded simply with "home" to the question *where* and with "Okay, I guess" to the question *What do you feel about it?*

Consider that response. It says a great deal about how your child sees him- or herself at that moment. Don't tell your child what else to take into consideration. If you want to explore what an answer means or to discover deeper feelings, ask what he or she means, without at the same time handing over the answer you want to hear. "Is that the only place you exist?" "What does okay feel like?" That kind of *nondirective* questioning will get you to a clearer understanding of how your child see things, of where the two of you are different.

But, you may protest, I'd just have wanted him or her to remember that he or she also exists in school.

Nondirective questioning will draw that answer out if the child is inclined to see him- or herself in school. If your child appears to avoid that response, it can be an important insight on your part to realize that as far as he or she is concerned, there is nothing to identify with at school. An effort on your part to give school a place in your child's self-identity it doesn't really have for him or her amounts to a refusal to recognize the difference here, unsettling as that may be.

You will have a great deal of difficulty trying to influence your child's development into a mature, responsible individual if you refuse to acknowledge your child's individuality—all those differences that add up to his or her way of seeing the world—from the very beginning.

In working with younger children, the Real You Collage can be useful, too. However, you will have to fill out the details based on your observations. Just trying for a few moments to imagine the world from your youngster's perspective can prove very valuable. That can lead to your realizing how different a place it appears to him or her and, consequently, why things are important to your child that are not important to you—and vice versa. The caution to keep in mind is that the profile you draw is still substantially influenced by the way you look at things.

## Value and Goal Differences

Once you've completed the Real You Collage exercise with your child, it should be obvious that what's important to the child is quite different from what's important to you. That will be so even if the underlying principle is the same.

Suppose both of you are very concerned about security. What that means to your child is certain to be very different from what that means to you. For instance, Joe, Jr.'s sense of security is probably closely tied to his experience of the home and the trust he places in his parents. Joe, Sr.'s will probably involve the home environment too, but from a radically different perspective; and he will probably think in terms of income, job security, and social position as well. Joe, Jr.'s sense of all that may be very limited or even nonexistent.

Children also have a comparatively undeveloped sense of time. Because they haven't had as much occasion to see the connection between past and present, they won't as readily understand the connection between present and future. You have a background of experience that prompts you increasingly to look at the long-range implications in the things you do. You generally realize that the actions of the present can have an effect far beyond the present. But children haven't had that lesson impressed upon them in the same way. In addition, the world is still a relatively new place for them. Their experiments and explorations aim at discovering how things work in the present and what's happening now. Their focus on the present leads them to favor choices that provide instant gratification. You'll be quicker to see other consequences that need to be taken into account.

Teaching your child to make well-considered decisions involves alerting him or her to the connection between present and future. Your objective is ultimately to have your child act independently in a mature, reasoned way. You will find many of your efforts toward that end stymied, however, if you don't at the same time take into account that your child doesn't see things your way and reacts to what he or she sees differently than you do.

Unless you begin with a sensitive awareness that your child's experience and needs cover a lot of considerations that aren't important to you, you won't be an effective teacher. Your efforts will be clumsy because you're trying to shape a personality that you only have a dim view of. You won't know how to build *from* who and where your child is now because you won't really know who and where he or she is now.

Values and goals are the heart of the decisionmaking process. If you are off-base in recognizing differences that exist between you and your child with respect to values and goals, you'll be unable to lead him or her into appreciating the benefit to be achieved from the process: an increased chance of influencing events to his or her advantage. Somehow decisionmaking may come to appear an instrument of parental control, a way of getting your child to do just what you think should be done. And therein lie the seeds of failure.

Parents have certain expectations for their children, and goals generally are based upon those expectations. Children may not be as concerned with those expectations as they are with a need to define their own place in the scheme of things. They have their own expectations; they are often as much influenced by the expectations of their peers, whose experience parallels theirs in obvious ways, as by the expectations of their parents.

Going after anything boils down to how one views the payoffs. As a parent, you have to begin with a recognition of your child's individuality, knowing why certain things are worth pursuing as far as your child is concerned.

Your chance of success does not depend on imposing your way of looking at things. It depends on a convincing demonstration that a systematic approach to choices, with a realistic consideration of consequences, will turn things to your child's advantage even when viewed from your child's perspective.

# 9

# Managing Differences

Wherever there are differences between people, there is potential for conflict. Since parents and their children will be quite dissimilar when it comes to interests, priorities, attitudes, skills, and abilities, even a good parent-child relationship will have its share of conflict. That of itself is no cause for distress. Unfortunately, parents often get very uneasy when differences between them and their children occasion disagreement, argument, or even a display of hostility.

The possibility of conflict puts parents into something of a double bind. On the one hand, you want your child to learn how to handle things on his or her own. On the other, you will have your own idea of what the best course of action is and realize he or she may not actually choose to follow it. You know there's a danger in trying to push your child toward a particular choice: He or she may well choose to do something else just to assert control over his or her own affairs, whatever the consequences.

In order to provide meaningful help, you first have to know how to defuse the possibility of conflict.

There's so much you can do along those lines. The idea is to keep your feelings and priorities from getting in the way of or distorting your ability to understand what your child is trying to say or do. You've got to make the effort to see things from your child's perspective in order for your involvement to be something more than interference. That means identifying what differences exist between you and your child and taking an approach that acknowledges those differences. We've begun that approach in the previous chapter. Now let's follow it through in terms of the decision framework.

### VALUES

Because any decision requires some kind of value-based judgment, it is vital you identify what is important to your child and why. What is the difference between that and what you think is important?

The Real You Collage in Chapter 8 provides one means of recognizing value differences and what lies behind them. Another way is through a comparative likes and dislikes inventory.

Write down as quickly as possible anything you truly enjoy doing. Include anything related to either work, leisure, or home life that provides you satisfaction. Then do the same for things you dislike. In corresponding columns to the right of your list, give yourself space to note whether others in your family share any of your likes or dislikes.

**A Comparative Likes/Dislikes Inventory**

| Things You Enjoy Doing | M. | F | Child | Similar (Why?) |
|---|---|---|---|---|
| _____ | ___ | ___ | _____ | _____ |
| _____ | ___ | ___ | _____ | _____ |
| _____ | ___ | ___ | _____ | _____ |
| _____ | ___ | ___ | _____ | _____ |
| _____ | ___ | ___ | _____ | _____ |
| _____ | ___ | ___ | _____ | _____ |

*Things You Don't Like*
  *to Do*

| | | | | |
|---|---|---|---|---|
| _____ | __ | __ | __ | _____ |
| _____ | __ | __ | __ | _____ |
| _____ | __ | __ | __ | _____ |
| _____ | __ | __ | __ | _____ |
| _____ | __ | __ | __ | _____ |
| _____ | __ | __ | __ | _____ |

Put a check in the columns headed *M, F,* and *Child* to indicate whether mother, father, and/or child share likes or dislikes in the activities listed. How many similarities did you discover? Why do those similarities exist? What accounts for any differences that exist? Are you in fact aware of what your child enjoys doing?

You can also tune in to differences between you and your child by focusing on happenings outside the family, if sorting them out within the family at first appears too difficult. Reactions to the news, to an article in a newspaper or magazine, to a movie, etc.—all provide indications of values held.

It's important you listen to value differences as expressed for an understanding of where they come from. You minimize the likelihood of conflict by considering that before you jump to conclusions about misbehavior.

Encourage your child to share his or her thoughts about what is and is not pleasing. Expand educational and other experiences so that he or she sees from a wider perspective in becoming aware of the influence of values. And encourage others in the family to share their views and feelings about what is or is not important to them. There will be many similarities to help you see that differences can be approached on a positive track.

GOALS

When an action is decided on, the results desired may not be clear to both parent and child. Besides that, the worth of the results may not be seen in the same way. Getting home on time may not be very important to the child involved in an exciting game with friends. In the meantime, the parent is worried sick. Likewise, picking up in one's room might not be worth the effort for the child, but it could a very important goal for the parent. Differences between what the child wants or thinks desirable and what the parent wants and thinks desirable easily lead to conflict.

It is in the nature of parenting to set goals for children, and this in particular leads to conflicts if not well handled. Parents often lay a goal on their child and then wonder later why there is no movement toward it on the part of the child. The difficulty is that the goal is not set in a way to encourage the child to adopt it as his or her own.

Movement toward anything requires advanced planning, unless one is content to live life more or less at random. To ensure your child works toward goals you at first set for him or her, you have to involve your child in planning how they are to be achieved.

## Goal Contracts

Think of goal achievement as something like a contract to be negotiated, with you in effect saying, "If you do this, you can count on me to do that." Make the goal one your child sees is within reach. Start with modest task-and-time plans that lead to something both sides want. Each success will open opportunities for achievement in related areas.

Any goal you negotiate and put into contract form should include specifics spelling out exactly:

*1.* What is wanted (goal)

2. The things to do to accomplish that (tasks)
3. The schedule for completion of tasks (time checks)
4. Indication of what success will mean (new opportunities)
5. The support required from others (parental tasks)
6. How you'll know the goal has been reached (what will happen)
7. How you'll celebrate achievement/completion (reward)

Keep in mind that this is an agreement between you and your child. Give your child the opportunity to contribute, so that the contract takes his or her priorities into account as well as yours.

You can apply the contract approach to the simplest of tasks, such as planning a birthday party, developing the work required for an allowance, deciding what to wear to school; or you can apply it to more complex situations, such as dating, curfew, grade achievement, personal appearance, college applications, etc. I have found it especially effective to put goal contracts on a big sheet of paper posted where everybody will see them and view them periodically. You can see what's involved by checking the sample goal contract provided.

Each goal success will tend to whet the appetite for doing something a little more ambitious the next time. Along the way, successes contribute to the child's sense of accomplishment and build self-esteem. They may, however, also contribute to a tendency to overreach oneself—to try to accomplish too many things at one time.

A mother came to me for guidance after her daughter had experienced several goal successes. It seemed that after each success the daughter wanted to take on even more. "I have so many things I want to do, I don't know where to begin. I want to improve my appearance [lose weight], make friends [reduce loneliness], and do better in school [improve grades]." The daughter's eagerness for further accomplishment was in fact leading to expressions of frustration.

While all of the goals expressed could be worked toward at

**Goal Contract**

*The contract of Thomas Miller*

| | |
|---|---|
| Result desired: | To get the best grades I can by completing all my work on time and completing homework as assigned. |
| Things to do: | 1. Keep assignment book up to date.<br>2. Remember to hand in assignments.<br>3. Get help in studying for tests. |
| What parent will do: | 1. Review tests and ask questions about the test material.<br>2. Help me in understanding my assignments.<br>3. Check homework once or twice a week. |
| Time schedule: | I will receive no bad interim reports for not doing my work during the first six weeks of the term. |
| Reward: | I will be able to make decisions on my own terms of deciding how much time I need to spend on my work.<br><br>I will be able to join the ice hockey team.<br><br>I will be able to watch television on Friday nights and Saturdays. |

Signed: _____

_____

the same time, I suggested setting up a staggered system for achievement, so that some progress would be evident in one area before others were worked on. That meant establishing goal priorities.

Mother and daughter subsequently identified weight loss as the most important goal, since it seemed to have some impact in areas in which other goals had been identified as well. They decided to pursue the weight loss goal for two weeks before setting up a plan for making new friends. Improving grades would be the last of the three goal areas planned for.

Setting goal priorities entails an exchange of ideas between parent and child so that subsequent planning clearly meets needs on both sides. That is extremely important for keeping conflict to a minimum.

Parents can also help resolve conflict that may arise as a result of obstacles encountered along the way to achieving goals. Most obstacles can be overcome in some way. It may simply be a matter of needing more time or taking a different approach. Assist your child in developing alternatives, always with an eye toward the child's seeing those as routes possible for achieving something he or she wants and will benefit from.

Don't treat goals as if they were set in concrete. Make it clear that as new information comes to light, they may need revision. That can mean lowering one's sights momentarily or identifying smaller steps that, over the course of time, still lead to the original goal.

If you do decide to follow a contractual approach, there may be times you'll have to tear up a contract.

A father whose son insisted on going out for his school's boxing team entered into a contract with him. It simply said that if the son went out for the team, he would have to stay with it for the season. They decided on this because the son had started so many things without completing them. But when his son returned home day after day with all kinds of bumps and bruises, the father suggested they reexamine their contract. Ultimately they concluded it would be best for the boy to withdraw from the boxing program.

### INFORMATION

Children come to view things differently from parents for reasons not always directly related to values and goals. Information differences are influential, too. Child and parent may have different information relating to a particular subject or interpret the same information in quite different ways.

Difference in point of view is always relevant. A teenager's decision to go steady promises one set of outcomes very important to him or her Those same outcomes may be viewed very negatively by the parent. As parent and child work on what to do after high school, it becomes apparent that the child sees the decision as "What should I do?" while the parent sees it as a matter of "What's the best college for my child?"

Value and goal differences will inevitably lead to reliance on different points and sources of information to build a case one way or other. Managing conflict here requires identifying what information differences exist and whether those are on the level of quality and quantity or relate to interpretation of the same facts. Interpretive differences have to be traced back to the value and goal difference(s) they arise from. The question of quantity and/or quality is more easily resolved by examining the information both sides have on the situation at hand.

When it comes to that, consider how information is passed along in the typical parent-child relationship. Good decisions hinge upon the use of timely and valid data. Unfortunately, in the exchange of information between parent and child, the parent is often at a disadvantage. Often key information is relayed only through the child, with the parent at a disadvantage to verify it.

For example, your daughter, Angela, wants to go to a party across town. She tells you all the other kids are going and that the rest of the parents have all said okay. Now, you trust Angela, and you feel the information she provides is probably accurate. What's missing? Well, to begin with, Angela has most likely received all her information from her friends. You don't know what the other parents actually said or why they approved. You also don't know, nor does Angela, how her friends actually got parent approval. The grant of permission may only have been something like "If all your friends are going, I guess it's okay for you to go, too."

The information flow can be diagrammed as below, with you the parent in an isolated position relative to all the others.

## Isolated Information Exchange

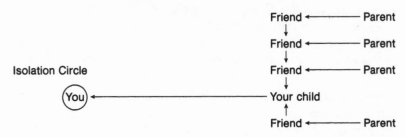

You can break out of the isolation circle in two ways. In this situation, an obvious remedy is to go directly to the other parents. More likely than not, you'll discover that most of them were not directly involved in the information exchange either. You know how it goes: "Gee, I was worried, too. The only reason I said Jeanne could go was because she said you had given your Angela permission to go."

Another effective way to break out of the isolation circle is to make information demands clear for any situation. In this case, you might ask who will be there, will there be adult supervision, will alcohol be served, is it an open party or one designed for just a few friends, and how does your child know all this? You're setting information minimums that must be filled in order to make an intelligent decision.

By no means is any of this a case of showing distrust for Angela. Rather, it's a case of needing a certain amount of information before agreement or disagreement is possible. It works to the benefit of Angela in an obvious way—she learns to fill information gaps before expecting approval. Similarly, she will feel free to question you when she is on the receiving end of information that puts her in the isolation circle.

As a parent, you may well find yourself in isolation when you deal with school officials, other parents, and your child's friends. In every case, your task is to move out of the isolation circle. Note how this comes about.

**Improved Information Exchange**

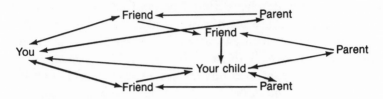

An improved information exchange is but part of your task here. You also want to be sure of getting *good* information. All too often parents rely on friends or just one identified "expert" for information. They don't take care to get all the information available, so subject themselves to the biases of only a few. To protect yourself against that, follow the guidelines in Chapter 5 for gathering and collating information.

Remember that brainstorming with all the family members involved in a decision is a good way to tune into information resources. Children often have good ideas about where and how to get information. This kind of brainstorming also does much to control conflict due to information differences, since it requires both parent and child to share the information they have.

### STRATEGIES

If you accept the notion that people naturally have different perspectives and learn and grow at different rates, then you must be willing to accept different strategies for getting to what is wanted. Conflict develops when parents fail to realize that children prefer to proceed at a rate and in a way that is comfortable and meaningful to them. Thus any plan for moving your children toward responsible independence requires a consideration of differences in needs, wants, readiness, and resources available.

A strategy is a plan or method for reaching a specific goal.

Normally, there are many different ways to reach the same objective, and it's here that the conflict potential exists. Choosing an appropriate strategy begins with knowing there are a number of means to an end and that each has its own risks and costs over both the short and the long term.

Normal family interactions and discussions provide excellent chances to become alert to options for establishing strategy. Both children and adults enjoy looking at outside situations to figure out what they would do in the same position. Taking a "what would you have done?" approach is an ideal skill-building exercise. You can do this with incidents reported in newspapers, local school happenings, and even television programs. The idea is to open up minds all around, to help your child in particular see that in most situations there are more options than there first appear to be. That's important, because children tend to move to the obvious when it comes to making choices, and that is precisely what you want to move them beyond.

The immediate next step once options are identified is to predict the possible and likely outcomes attached to each. It's a case of moving from "What would you do?" to "What might happen if you did it?" No option should ever be chosen without a careful consideration of the short- and long-term consequences that might follow. And a final selection should come only after all options and their outcomes have been identified and compared (unless you need to keep alternatives manageable; then follow the guidelines in Chapter 4).

Here's an example of how to go about comparing options: A teenager is faced with the decision of what to do after high school.

As you can see, if you approach the outcomes of each option creatively, you can compare positives and negatives in related areas. In the example above, I've sketched out only two of the possible options fully. In any situation facing you and your

| Option | Outcome possible | Outcome likelihood | Information gaps |
|---|---|---|---|
| Go to college | Prep for job | Likely | What is employment picture? |
| | Expensive | Likely | Scholarship/financial aid possibilities? |
| | Not like it | Not likely | How do I know this? |
| | Meet new people | Likely | |
| Work and go to college part-time | | | |
| Travel for a year | | | |
| Military service | Prep for job | Likely | What job prep? |
| | Earn and learn | Likely | |
| | Travel | Likely | Travel guarantee? |
| | Meet new people | Likely | |
| | Danger potential | Not likely | What are the possibilities of combat? |
| Get married | | | |
| Go to technical school | | | |

child, you would of course draw lines of comparison between all those under consideration.

By helping your child sketch out a decision this way, you'll both see where information needs lie. As you fill in the gaps, you'll be able to make well-informed comparisons that will make the child more confident about the final choice. All too often this process never takes place because the young person goes with the obvious and the parent goes along with that. At times that is virtually the same as making no conscious decision.

For example, if a child goes to college or to work without comparing that alternative to others, there's really been no conscious selection among alternatives. The child has forfeited the chance to review the relative advantage of one option over another. A common result of this is a feeling after a decision has been made that one doesn't really know why he decided on what he did. It's not necessarily that the choice made was a bad one, just that there was no effort to confirm that it was a good one and why.

Clearly, this part of making decisions requires exploring all the possibilities seriously. Parents must encourage this exploration, even though it can be unnerving to do so at times. You may think college is the best option and therefore prove reluctant to introduce other possibilities for consideration: "My God, what if she chooses military service?"

Well, keep things in perspective. The bottom line is arriving at a good decision. The option chosen must stand up to evaluation as the best course available, given the values, goals, risks, and costs involved on the part of the person deciding. If in fact the choice is for military service, you too will be able to see how that best ties in with your child's needs and values. Provided you accept your child's right to express those in her own life, you will find yourself more readily accepting the decision she makes.

Once an option has been selected, a full-blown plan can be developed for following through to reach the goal that's been set. This plan should specify:

- What the objective pursued is and when that is to be achieved.
- The steps required to pursue the option selected.
- The responsibility and time limit for completing each step.
- The standards established for each step.
- The resources allocated for each step—time, energy, money, etc.
- A prediction of possible difficulties and contingency plans to meet those should they materialize.

Once the plan is at the stage of implementation, the original goal, steps taken to achieve it, and progress made should be reviewed, so that revisions can be made as necessary.

A strategy can be as simple or complex as a person wants to make it, but either way, your child will need help developing plans. You can head off problems by taking the time to work through the planning suggestions provided here. Whatever you do, exercise patience. Your child may have good reasons for proceeding differently than you might. Give him or her a chance to develop and think through the strategy he or she feels most comfortable with.

### USE THE DECISION FRAMEWORK

The decision framework is perhaps the best way to manage differences effectively. While it can be time-consuming, it tends to have the greatest success when it comes to reducing or eliminating conflict about choices of action. Some uncomfortable moments may arise, because it does encourage a head-on examination of differences, but those have to be recognized and acknowledged sooner or later anyway. And as a shared, supportive learning experience, it helps both parent and child learn and grow.

Any number of questions can serve to keep differences in manageable perspective. Some of the best are:

- What does my child hope to accomplish in this situation, and how does this differ from what I want him or her to accomplish?
- Why does my child want to accomplish this?
- What information, either factual or related to feelings, do I need in order to understand my child's behavior?
- What course of action is my child considering for getting the results desired?
- Are there better ways to go about getting what is desired?
- What can I do to help my child find and consider these ways?

As you can see, these questions force you to highlight the needs, wants, and priorities both you and your child bring to the situation. In addition, they orient you to a search for alternative courses of action that may be more appropriate for meeting those needs, wants, and priorities. By identifying the decision and considering all aspects of it, you provide a nonconfronting framework for locating and defining differences, which can be resolved through the joint effort of seeking out the best alternative for taking action. That does much to head off open, destructive conflict.

### Guidelines for Neutralizing Conflict

When using the decision framework, incorporate these attitudes and behaviors into your line of approach:

1. *Treat differences as normal occurrences in your relationship with your child.* Let your child see that his or her uniqueness as an individual is acceptable and respected in the home.

2. *Listen before evaluating.* Frustration and conflict increase whenever one feels he or she is not being heard. Listen so you can spot and assess differences early and accurately.

3. *Focus on the nature of the conflict.* Where differences give rise to conflict, the cost can quickly run high for all concerned. You as a parent must be quick to understand what is happening and why, so that you can identify emerging conflict as soon as possible. The earlier you identify conflict, the easier it is to keep within limits and then resolve.

4. *Provide an opportunity for your child to vent feelings.* Feelings that go unnoticed or are kept hidden tend to fester and grow, then explode into a high level of open conflict. You can reduce the chance that hard feelings will erupt into unexpected conflict by expressing openly how you feel and allowing your child to do the same.

5. *Designate who is responsible for a decision, and make sure there are clear boundaries defining the decider's limits of action.* There should be no conflict possible later because somehow

the rules of the game were not understood. Your child must know his or her limits and the consequences for violating those.

6. *Develop alternatives with your child so he or she does not feel trapped by the false notion that there is no other way to proceed.* Even if there is no other way, the reasons for pursuing the option taken should be expressed clearly.

7. *Establish feedback opportunities and set standards for evaluating progress made in resolving differences.* This also sets up a means for keeping tabs on any conflict being generated in the course of implementing the decision made.

8. *Help your child identify the decision elements that could put differences in clearer perspective.* Are value differences behind disagreement with your way of looking at things? Is it a matter of different goals? Is it a question of information discrepancy or of pursuing a strategy that is not clear or varies from one you might follow?

Any important decision is likely to point up some differences between parent and child. Differences aren't necessarily bad. In fact, they can prove stimulating and exciting, make life truly interesting. But if differences give rise to full-blown conflict, the result will be painful and perhaps destructive for all those involved. Applying the decision framework enables you to pick up early warning signals of conflict and to work through differences with your child so you both recognize what the best course of action is.

Many parents try to manage differences by ignoring them as much as possible. While looking the other way may be a convenient way to deal with differences in the short term, it does not help a parent see what's involved in those. It doesn't help head off any conflict that may emerge. In fact, looking the other way is likely to result in conflict that is more intense and hard to manage when it does surface.

Other parents take an "I'm telling you what to do!" approach. But telling, in the absence of listening to and responding to differences, does not provide children a framework for resolving conflict. It does little to promote independence and the ability to think for oneself and come up with new alternatives that accommodate individual differences.

Applying the decision framework to manage differences in the home is part of the total effort necessary to creation of a home environment that stimulates growth toward independent responsibility. In the next chapter, I'll provide you guidelines for keeping open lines of communication, building trust, and formulating a clear family philosophy with defined limits on acceptable behavior. Following the guidelines there will do much to ensure that differences don't build up to misunderstanding and avoidable conflict.

# 10

# Creating a Positive Home Environment

When it comes to teaching children decisionmaking skills, there's truly no place like home. Home is where your child begins the long process of establishing his or her own identity and sense of place in the general scheme of things. Home is where your child first encounters the possibilities of choice and learns something about consequences, the stuff decisions grow out of. Consider, too, that many children are kept at home for the first years of life. It provides them nearly their only frame of reference for judging how to relate to the rest of the world.

Virtually all theories of child development assume a pattern of movement from dependence to independence. The process begins with the young child at home accepting authority and behaving obediently. What adults say goes. However, acceptance is soon replaced, at least in part, by questioning, and the child learns to act more on his or her own. A behavior pattern begins to emerge, with the child achieving things alone and in his or her own way to the extent possible. Gradually the child matures to the point where he or she also starts recognizing others' points of view and takes them into account in his or her own behavior.

Maturing, in this case, means moving toward responsible behavior—going beyond oneself to routinely take the welfare of others into account. Because the home is the primary setting in the child's life, it follows that the best insurance of movement to maturity is the parents' willingness and readiness to teach responsible behavior in the home. That requires careful attention and applied effort on their part.

Parents must be aware of the child's needs and of the child's abilities as these develop. They must be prepared to intervene at times. They must take the lead in helping the child gain self-confidence, respect the rights of others, and make and carry out well-considered decisions.

Implicit in all this is that parents are in a natural position of power over their children. At least they start out that way. Unfortunately, contemporary society has introduced a variety of complications that affect family life. Parents have less time to concentrate energies on concerns of the home, with a host of distractions vying for attention when it comes to putting what time remains to good use. In many instances, parents have come to rely on others to provide their children necessary guidance—leaving that up to the schools, religious groups, and/or the government. As a result, they have forfeited their power and grown out of touch with their children's needs and problems.

Study after study has found meaningful parent interaction time with children to be almost nonexistent. One study of middle-class fathers found they spent about six seconds per day in close contact with their children who were less than a year old. Six seconds!

Time, which is more and more precious for adults wrestling with survival in an uncertain world, is not being treated as the priceless commodity that it is. What time is available is not put to constructive use in the home and so has little impact in promoting responsible behavior in children. But so far, there's little evidence that the task of inspiring responsible behavior can be handled well on a routine basis outside the family. Parents who give up their power to others find themselves nevertheless having to deal with the problems and difficulties that grow out of immature behavior on the part of their children. In order to do so effectively, they have to reclaim their power and learn to exert that constructively.

A vital part of the constructive use of power is creating a positive home environment that encourages the development of responsible behavior. Experience shows that this requires attention to several basic considerations: effective communication between parent and child, mutual trust, an explicit family philosophy with defined limits of acceptable behavior. Attention to these ensures that the procedure for identifying and responding to differences within the family works satisfactorily. And that's as true for building on the positives as for keeping the negatives under control.

### EFFECTIVE COMMUNICATION

Effective communication is at the base of most relationships. It is characterized by an open dialogue between the two sides, with as much emphasis on listening as on talking. It stimulates sharing, a sense of mutual support, and mutual respect.

Poor communication leads to misunderstandings, hurt feelings, a loss of self-respect, conflict, and poor decisionmaking. Where parents rely heavily on yelling, commanding, and sarcasm to relay messages to their children, the parent-child relationship is commonly a strained one. The parents' unwillingness to listen to their children's expressions of need and feeling usually boomerangs—the children then prove just as unwilling to take the parents' needs and feelings into account.

Because communication is a two-way process, both parent and child must work at developing effectiveness in this area. You can help your child by adopting communication habits that provide a good model to follow. While at times you may find yourself insisting your child make the effort to communicate with you, that is much less often necessary than you might think. A block in communications between parent and child is very often relieved simply by the parent's taking a new initiative. As the child sees an increased readiness to take his needs, feelings, observations, and experiences into account, he is more likely to share those with you. He is also more likely to take your perspective into account.

Improved communication is a relatively simple matter, but it is not necessarily an easily achieved goal. Old habits must be broken, and habits are often difficult to break. Both parent and child must work hard to be open in situations where in the past the tendency has been to shut the other person up or out. Otherwise there is little chance of developing the give and take required to address the needs of both sides. Give and take is necessary to preserve and promote self-respect, a basic prerequisite for a positive experience of life and a positive view of the choices one faces in life.

### Listening

Listening is the first phase of good communication. It yields the information needed to move from not understanding to recognizing meaning in words and behavior.

Good listening goes beyond hearing the obvious; it goes beyond hearing altogether. Observation plays a major part, too. What your child says with "body language" can be as significant as the precise words chosen. What stance does your child take when speaking to you? Does he or she seem tense? Is your child looking at or away from you? Is the face pinched or taut? Is he or she fidgeting with his or her hands? Is your child listless, animated, calm, or excited? Does he or she seem on the edge of tears? And as for what you're hearing, note the tone of voice as well as the content of the words spoken. Do they seem to match?

Keep in mind that your body language also says much about you as a listener. If you are sincerely attentive, you will automatically incline your body toward the child, face him or her fully, and maintain regular eye contact. (That is not the same as an unremitting gaze, the intensity of which can be intimidating and so impede communication.) Observe yourself from time to time. What do your attitudes and body language tell your child when he or she tries to communicate with you?

Develop good listening habits. Nothing else you do will contribute as much to improved communication with your child.

*Set up a reason for listening.* Your interactions with your child provide a constant flow of information, not all of which you can manage in a lump. By knowing what information you're looking for, you'll be able to focus on what is most immediate and/or important and interpret and respond to that more easily and appropriately.

*Be nonjudgmental; just listen.* It's often tempting to jump into the thick of things very quickly with a lot of probing questions or pointed statements reflecting your view of things. Resist the temptation, or you'll wind up doing all the talking. Then your child will either go on the defensive or clam up, and you won't find out what is on his or her mind.

*Resist distractions.* When you and your child have something important to talk about, have your discussion where you won't be interrupted or distracted. Turn off the TV or radio; tell other people to leave you alone for a while. And give yourself time for the interaction, not just a couple hurried minutes during which you have your eye on the clock.

*Keep in mind that the first problem introduced may not be the real one.* Very often your child will state a concern that is not really at the heart of the issue. That makes it important to suspend initial judgments and listen so you're sure you're dealing with the real problem. For example, your son Peter may tell you he wants to quit his Little League team, saying he doesn't like the sport, when actually he is trying to figure out how to deal with an abusive coach.

*Watch for commonalities.* Important themes will generally be repeated with some intensity. Listen for repetitions, and pay attention to your child's tone of expression for an indication of the feelings being communicated.

*Point out inconsistencies.* As you listen, you may note some contradictions the child is not aware of. Bring these to his or her attention. It may help to focus on the real issue. But don't keep hammering at the contradictions in a way that puts your child on the defensive. Observe their appearance, remark on them, but put off any confrontation that might develop. See at first if your child recognizes contradictions in what he or she says and the reaction to having them pointed out to him or her.

*Try to imagine yourself in your child's situation.* The point is, after all, to understand as best you can what your child is telling you, and that means stepping outside yourself for a moment to the degree possible. Ask yourself:

- What do I think my child is thinking?
- What do I think he or she is feeling?
- What do I think his or her intentions are?
- What do his or her actions mean?
- What's really bothering him or her?

These questions help guard against your overriding everything with an effort to impose your view of the situation before you've even given your child a chance to explain his or her view.

### Responding

This is the second phase of communication. Basically, a good response means you have listened to and understood your child's message.

There are two levels of response. On one level, you try to clarify or ensure your understanding. On the other, you move to throw into focus your child's feelings about what's being said. Psychologists term responses at the first level *cognitive*, and those at the second level *affective*.

There are four response patterns to employ. The first two aim at ensuring you correctly heard or understood what was said (they are cognitive responses); the third and fourth aim at identifying the child's reaction to what he or she is reporting (they are affective responses).

1. *Repetition.* This is a simple response that gives you time to think and double-check that what you heard was what your child said.

> *Child*:  I think I'm stupid.
> *Parent*:  You think you're stupid.

2. *Restatement or paraphrase.* Here you summarize the content of the child's statement as you understand it.

> *Child*:  I wish Ellen wasn't moving away.
> *Parent*:  You and Ellen are good friends, and you're going to miss her.

3. *Extrapolation of feelings behind words.* You identify the feelings you sense behind what the child says. Here you're going beyond simple content to understanding the total picture more clearly.

> *Child*:  I hate it when the teacher makes me stand up in front of the class when I don't know the answer.
> *Parent*:  That must be terribly embarrassing for you.
> *Child*:  Yeah, I feel like such a jerk.
> *Parent*:  You must really dislike the teacher when that happens.
> *Child*:  I sure do.

4. *Interpretation.* Here you identify how the child experiences him- or herself within the context of his or her world. That requires an understanding of both the content of what's said and the feelings behind it.

*Child*:   I really don't like those parties when there's a lot of drinking and stuff going on.

*Parent*:   You feel a lot of pressure to do what everyone else is doing.

*Child*:   Yeah.

*Parent*:   Sometimes we all question whether it's worth it to do what we know is right.

*Child*:   It's hard to say no.

*Parent*:   You feel it's unfair that you even have to worry about saying no.

*Child*:   Yeah, especially when some of my friends are doing it.

*Parent*:   You feel your friends have let you down.

*Child*:   Yes.

*Parent*:   Well, you didn't let yourself down.

*Child*:   No, and I'm glad about that.

*Parent*:   Maybe it will be easier to say no the next time.

*Child*:   You know, I was thinking the same thing.

The idea is to develop responses that consider your child's feelings and concerns and avoid making judgments. That will open the door to full disclosure of a situation and, in the process, convince your child that you are both listening and making the effort to understand as best you can.

Examples of good responses are:

- "You seem very disappointed."
- "It must have been a tough day for you."
- "They must have hurt your feelings a lot."
- "Things like that are hard to figure out."
- "You'd like to be able to avoid that situation."
- "You have trouble saying no."
- "You'd like to feel you can count on people."

Examples of responses to avoid include:

- "I knew that would happen."
- "How could you do such a thing?"

- "That was the wrong thing to do."
- "How can you treat people that way!"
- "I don't see why you're so upset over a little thing like this."
- "Why don't you act more like your brother?"
- "You're just going to have to work harder."

You may be thinking that in discussion with your child you want him or her to see when a poor decision was made. Well, that's exactly why you should avoid pushing that conclusion on him or her. When you label a situation or action with an immediate judgment of your own, you deprive your child of the opportunity to develop his or her own insight into the behavior. Your child won't see that a poor decision was made. All that will be apparent is that *you* think your child made a poor decision. You haven't given him or her the chance to personally figure that out. And, of course, you won't have given yourself a chance to test your own first conclusion. It's possible you may not have understood the situation fully or appreciated the difficulty it presents your child.

Pay attention to how you communicate with your child. Practice an open style. Have other adults tell you something about your body language, tone of voice, and how you generally make people feel when responding to their efforts to win your attention and understanding. Listen to yourself on a tape recorder to get a measure of your normal, unstressed tone of voice. Then, when communicating with your child, find out how he or she sees your reactions, your point of view, and your willingness to listen.

**TRUST**

Trust is another essential. It is not wholly separate—none of these essentials are. You go a long way toward developing trust when you make the effort to communicate effectively. And similarly, you ensure more effective communication as you display attitudes that contribute to developing trust.

Understand that trust is more than having confidence in someone's willingness or ability to perform in a certain way. It is much broader. The trust I am talking about is basic to the establishment of a secure self-identity in relationships with others. It particularly includes confidence in oneself, which grows out of a clear sense of place in the general scheme of things. For children, trust helps them respond positively to such questions as:

- How do I see myself in this family?
- How do others see me?
- How do I want others to see me?

The attitudes you must show to establish trust are acceptance, understanding, caring, honesty, tolerance, flexibility, and supportiveness.

Let's look at what's involved in each case.

### Acceptance

In its simplest terms, acceptance means letting your child know he or she has a right to his or her own thoughts, feelings, and actions. You express a willingness to let your child discover his or her own identity and a readiness to live with the differences that includes.

Differences prove very threatening to many parents. But in the real world, it is unlikely that any two people, even in the same family, will develop and change in exactly the same manner or at the same rate.

Differences are bound to exist. Approached positively, they can prove stimulating to all involved. Differences supply a change of pace. They give family members new ways of looking at things. They encourage understanding and tolerance when it comes to deviation from the norm.

Behaving according to one's own sense of things is not the same as being selfish. On the contrary, it is often a very healthy signal indicating the child has begun to find himself or herself and has gained enough confidence to go after what seems really important. While a parent can expect to experience some anxiety as differences become apparent, working to discourage them can be a serious mistake. Sooner or later all children have to learn to live with themselves. That means accepting their own uniqueness and not always trying to live a parental definition of what they should be and do.

Differences in this context have nothing to do with establishing what is right or wrong in a moral or ethical sense. As a parent, it is up to you to establish guidelines and procedures for your children when it comes to what is ethically right or wrong. What we're talking about here are differences relating to personal priorities, goals, and a readiness to take risks. Your child has a right to establish personal standards in these areas, and differences are to be expected. You might not choose to do things the same way, but then you're a different person.

Acceptance requires you to look beyond your initial anxiety or misgivings. You can make that easier on yourself by taking a good look at yourself and seeing and accepting *your* difference from others. Observe how differently you behave than your own parents, for example.

Then look for ways to show your acceptance of your child. Don't try to force your priorities; let your child identify and respond to his or her own.

A good example of nonaccepting parental behavior can be found on the Little League athletic field. You know the scene—parents purple with frustration, screaming at their children to win, to run faster, to knock somebody down. Yesteryear's "tiger" finds it hard to imagine his child not approaching a game the way he did. Refusal to accept the difference leads to predictable results: the child tends to give up trying to participate in competitive situations, and a sense of strain develops as an outgrowth of the parent's frustrated expectations.

In the same situation, the accepting parent seeks to build on the child's efforts to establish himself or herself in the competitive environment. This parent looks for improvements and accentuates the positive, thereby leading the child into a more enjoyable experience. The parent is also spared considerable frustration.

### Understanding

Understanding literally means putting yourself in your child's place. It's accomplished through becoming a good listener and learning to respond with an awareness of the child's feelings in preference to imposing your own view of things. The point is to develop a sense of empathy so you know, to the extent you can, what your child is thinking and feeling.

Understanding and acceptance go hand in hand. The more you are able to understand, the easier it will be to accept the difference in how your child behaves compared to how you might behave.

### Caring

Accepting and understanding will do much to show you care. However, it takes something more. You must demonstrate a willingness to act when situations call for that. The willingness to act is evident in reaching out to your child, getting information on his or her needs, listening, and following through to check on progress. Sticking to consequences or taking disciplinary action are also examples of caring when done with your child's best interests at heart, and your child will see them as such.

### Honesty

Honesty simply means being on the level. It includes sharing what is important to you in terms of both facts and feelings. It also means admitting you don't know all the answers, so that then you're able to look for those answers with your child.

Consistency between what you say and do is a major part of how your child will measure your honesty. Make no mistake: as a parent you are an example whose behavior is constantly observed. Your child is naturally concerned with whether or not you are leveling with him or her. Lack of consistency brings your honesty into question and impedes the development of trust between you and your child.

## Tolerance

There's a close link between tolerance and acceptance. However, there's also a distinction I feel is important.

Acceptance, as we've seen, basically confirms your child's right to a separate identity and differences growing out of his or her uniqueness as an individual. Tolerance here refers to a readiness to allow your child freedom of action to do things on his or her own initiative and independently.

You must allow your child a certain freedom if you mean to prepare him or her for responsible independence. Otherwise he or she has no room for developing decisionmaking skills. Logically, the right to freedom increases with the demonstration that your child is able to use it constructively.

Here's where the link between tolerance and acceptance is so important. It's essential that you realize that the determination of whether or not freedom has been used constructively depends on the effect on the child personally, *not* on whether he or she has done with it what you would have done under the same or similar circumstances.

In the end, the amount of freedom you accord your child should correspond with the evidence provided of an ability to make well-considered choices, without your insisting all the choices follow your sense of program.

### Flexibility

Parents have to set rules and outline procedures to be followed in the home. There's no way around that, nor need there be a concern to find one. But rules and procedures should not be engraved in stone to apply forever to all circumstances. They should be flexible enough so that when circumstances change it's possible to accommodate that change positively.

Your reasons for setting limits or standards in the home should be clear. However, they will inevitably be questioned from time to time. Respond to questions with an open mind. Be ready to reevaluate a limit or a set way of doing things that may no longer work to best advantage. Take into account that modifying limits is also an indication of growing faith in your child's ability to handle affairs independently. It's through your allowing change that he or she learns there's a payoff for more mature behavior.

### Supportiveness

While all of the above attitudes are supportive in some way, real support involves you as a parent helping your child work through situations. It is particularly evident where you prove willing to help correct a mistake your child has made and to bolster him or her as he or she wrestles with the consequences of that mistake.

Support does not mean forgetting about the consequences of your child's action. Instead, it means showing continued love and a readiness to help your child learn to avoid making the same mistake again.

The supportive parent gets involved, not just after the fact, but as soon as a difficult situation is identified.

The ideal helping atmosphere begins with establishing a setting in the home where you have the best chance of discovering why your child is doing something. At the same time, you become an active partner in working through dilemmas facing him or her.

All the attitudes that contribute to trust come into play here. Your child gains confidence in you and builds self-confidence at the same time. Your child learns how and why he or she is accountable for personal actions. You child begins to see other points of view and is able to take them into account. Your child learns to distinguish between responsible, constructive behavior and behavior that is irresponsible and destructive; your child comes to recognize the value of a choice for the former over the latter.

## A CLEARLY STATED FAMILY PHILOSOPHY

Most parents think they know where they are coming from and why on issues that affect or involve the family. Young people are less clear on things. They do not automatically understand why parents think or feel as they do.

Achieving trust and being responsive to your child as events unfold help to clarify your position on things, but something more is needed. Your philosophy and the why's of your positions must be openly expressed. That way all family members know where the family stands and why. Then each difficulty that arises can be worked through with minimal confusion or conflict, and with far less expenditure of energy.

A family philosophy is a general framework for thinking about things, for placing them in perspective, and for understanding why certain behavior is or is not acceptable. It focuses on why things are important and why family members, the parents in particular, take certain actions. It should take individual differences into account and be able to accommodate change if it is to serve the entire family's needs over a period of time.

Underlying any family philosophy should be a well-established set of values that provide the rationale for standards

that family members live and work by. The attitudes, expectations, priorities, and rules that operate in the family setting
should be consistent with and understandable through the
family philosophy. Because each family is unique and operates
in different settings and under different conditions, each family philosophy can be expected to differ from others in some
areas.

A philosophy for any family will cover areas such as

- Behavior toward adults
- Respect for and treatment of siblings
- Individual freedom
- Physical health
- Personal hygiene and appearance
- School or work performance
- Social contacts
- Citizenship or community outlook

You can go further to specific guidelines in areas like curfews
and gift-giving, depending on your sense of need for explicit
understanding there.

The family philosophy is made up of statements that consider the objectives and values of the family, the procedures for
daily living, and the rules established in the family or society.
Once you identify objectives, your statement of philosophy
should suggest how family members share responsibility, how
decisions will be made, and how independence will be earned.
Through attention to these considerations, your family philosophy will make clear relationships both among family members and with the outside world. It will set goals and suggest
ways to reach those goals.

Does this mean you should actually sit down and write out a
family philosophy? Well, it's not absolutely necessary, but I do
recommend it as an exercise in developing awareness and
checking consistency. Many parents manage to set out a clear
and consistent family philosophy without committing that to
paper, but it's probably more common to find parents setting

standards for unclear reasons and applying them unevenly. That contributes to confusion and resentment in children. It also makes it difficult to define or measure progress.

Taking time to draft a clear statement eliminates most of these problems. It also provides parents a more evident set of guidelines for evaluating situations and behaviors that involve their children. The parents as well as the children have a more secure sense of how to react to developments within or affecting the family.

How do you go about formulating a family philosophy? Begin by identifying goals or objectives. What do you think is desirable or acceptable in areas such as are listed above? Think in terms of behavior. For example, in considering citizenship, your statement of philosophy might read something like this:

CITIZENSHIP: We believe participation in activities with a community focus promotes a positive relationship with others in the world around us. It provides us the opportunity to understand and respect the differences of others while gaining acceptance and respect for ourselves as unique individuals.

Family members should spend time each week in a group activity that promotes a community-related outlook. As a family unit, we feel active support of our church is particularly important, with each family member participating in a church group set up for his or her age category. We feel participation in community groups outside the church is important, too. For the children, we encourage membership in scouting organizations, extracurricular school activities, or youth branches of community service organizations.

Each child may choose what to participate in, provided he or she attends conscientiously to home and schoolwork responsibilities. Group activities must be under adult supervision.

When formulating a family philosophy, allow each family member an opportunity to present his or her perspective. Again, keep in mind that it will be necessary to revise guidelines as changes occur—as your children learn more about themselves and their relationship to others, as you learn more about your children's growing capabilities and needs, and as you each find it advisable or necessary to adjust to changes in the world around you.

Don't make the mistake of assuming that your family philosophy, once established, has to remain fixed for all time and in application to every circumstance.

### SETTING LIMITS ON BEHAVIOR

The family philosophy, defining as it does what behavior is acceptable and what is not, makes it possible to set limits on behavior that are clear to all. It must be clear that all family members are accountable for their actions. That means that all must face up to the consequences that attach to their actions.

Unfortunately, parents generally do a poor job of developing consequences *in advance of* their child's decision to engage in a particular line of behavior. This creates confusion and uneasiness. The child cannot take consequences into account in deciding on an action, because those have not yet been established. So the child fails to see the connection between his or her decision and parental reaction to that. It is not clear that the decision invited the reaction. Rather, the reaction will be seen as something arbitrarily decided on as a result of the parent's mood at the moment.

As children grow, they are constantly testing, trying to determine how they fit into the scheme of things. It's their way of learning about limits—about what's possible and not possible, about what provides benefits and what doesn't. If limits on behavior are not clearly defined, your child may come to believe it's all right to try anything and that his or her own interpretation of results is all that matters. A home environment that seems to support those conclusions encourages reckless, irresponsible experimentation outside the home as well. Your child will turn to peers rather than to you for a definition of what's all right in a given set of circumstances. That leads to an easy disregard for limits altogether, since it will be characteristic of peer group members all to be testing those continually.

Parents in the last decade have tended to deemphasize consequences connected with irresponsible behavior, and this at a time of rapid social change and increasing uncertainty in the world at large. The result has been a generation of young people unsure of what is acceptable and what is not. A kind of value-less atmosphere has been allowed to develop in the average home and, by extension, in contemporary society. The feeling has increasingly come to be that there should be no limits and that anything is okay.

But everything has consequences. It's evident in the lack of meaning or purpose in the lives of many young people today that they've suffered from not being obliged to accept responsibility for the choices they've made. They've encountered limits imposed by reality and proved unprepared to deal with or accept those. They've failed to comprehend that limits are part of the natural order of things.

All the research I've studied indicates that children as a rule really want the structure that defined limits provide. They may complain at times, but structure takes a lot of pressure off them, especially in difficult decision situations. They're provided clear cues on behavior; they don't have to deal with uncontrolled situations.

Don't confuse limits with a lack of trust or with a low opinion of your child's ability to take independent action. See them rather as guards against the prospect of your child getting into situations where he or she has no control or cannot escape from possible dangers or difficulties. For example, my wife and I trusted our teenage daughter completely with regard to her social decisions and had no fear about her ability to act responsibly on her own. However, we did not allow her to go to unchaperoned parties. An unchaperoned situation presents possibilities over which a child, even if responsible, will not have control—party crashers, excessive alcohol consumption, property damage due to others' rowdy behavior, etc.

Clear limits also provide a framework for response to unacceptable behavior. When consequences are clearly established in advance, your child expects to pay a price for violating limits. You don't have to go through irritating explanations and negotiations each time unacceptable behavior occurs.

> Fifteen-year-old Karen called her parents from a party asking to stay longer. Her parents had established 10:30 P.M. as the time limit for leaving. They had also made clear that failure to observe the limit would result in curtailed social activity. In this instance, Karen's parents would not yield on the limit they'd established. (Yielding on limits can undermine them so that they become meaningless.) Karen was quite upset and became very abusive when she got home. Her parents simply asked her if she was aware of the limits that had been established. She was. They then pointed out that her behavior was inconsistent with the family philosophy as it related to the situation at hand. Through her behavior she was in effect telling them she was not ready to behave responsibly.

As a child becomes more responsible, certain limits will require adjustment, but this adjustment must be based on new needs and evidence of additional skills he or she has developed. Discuss limits and consequences with your child from time to time, and arrive at adjustments through mutual understanding. Help your child understand what is required in order for limits to be lifted or modified in some way.

Once you've established limits, you should not change them unless:

1. *An adjustment in specifics is necessary or further explanation is called for.* For example, assigned tasks around the home may not be negotiable, but it may prove desirable or possible to carry them out at different times and to a different level of standard.

2. *The facts in a situation change.* Facts are objective pieces of information and not to be confused with opinions or arguments. The reason for setting clear limits to begin with is to reduce the need to negotiate what's acceptable and what's not acceptable in every set of circumstances that entails some choice of action.

*3. Goals have been reached or objectives accomplished earlier than anticipated.* If something has been done satisfactorily before a given deadline, obligations have been met and rewards can be given at the actual completion date.

*4. It is clear that the original consequence does not make sense or hold up over time.* Either parents or the child may suggest revision when this proves the case.

The consequences you establish for behavior must be consistent with the family philosophy, should be *mutually* established and revised (that is, with both parents and child having a chance to express their point of view), and must be honored by both parents and child.

A consistent emphasis on consequences is the only way to orient your child to the connection that always exists between a decision to act and what happens as the result of that decision. It's absolutely essential for building a sense of accountability and responsibility within the family and in relation to society at large.

# PART III

# Parenting Toward Independence

---

Although your child may be as old as twelve or fifteen, so that you will think to look at the information in Chapter 14 or 15 for guidance on helping him or her with decisions, you will do best to review material presented in the earlier chapters of this section as well. Earlier chapters discuss attitudes and techniques that may have had or can have substantial influence on your child's development and on your relationship with your child. To best help your child, it is important you tune into past patterns of behavior. In addition, a number of techniques introduced for parenting in the early years will prove of use, even if by now your child is a junior high or high school student.

# 11

# The Preschool Child—Setting a Pattern

Decisionmaking becomes part of a child's life as soon as he or she begins to understand the difference between *yes* and *no*. Even though the parents may not recognize that anything like a conscious selection of alternatives is taking place, it is at this point that the child learns to connect choices with consequences. The alternatives may be very limited—to cooperate or not to cooperate, to obey or disobey. The connection to be drawn between the attitude expressed and what happens as a result is nevertheless very important.

In the first years of life, children take most of their cues on behavior from their parents. Preschool youngsters tend to be very accepting; they take most of what the parents suggest or demonstrate as an indication of how the world in general operates. But this is also a period of great discovery and experimentation. They begin to sense power in themselves somewhere. They test limits. They start to say no, as a way of asserting their own budding sense of individuality and also to check out the parents' response. It's in these early years that your reactions combine into a general pattern that will likely affect you and the child for years to come.

At this point in your child's life, you will constantly be called upon to respond to how he or she feels. Even at age two or three, your child is filing away certain observations about you for future reference. Your responses provide the sense of consequences that come to be associated with various acts and behaviors. And these are directly connected to developing habits that may be characteristic of your child over a lifetime.

## THE INFLUENCE OF PARENTAL ATTITUDES

### *The Importance of a Positive Approach*

The way you respond to your preschool child's behavior has a profound influence on his or her developing sense of self-worth. It's all too easy to start a child down a road of negativity. If you fail to emphasize the positive in setting or reaffirming consequences, reacting only to what you see as not good enough or wrong, you may well contribute to your child's drawing the conclusion that he or she cannot act capably.

Naturally you have to set clear limits and establish explicit consequences to prompt your child into acceptable behavior. That's a fundamental parental task. But be sure that from the beginning you provide recognition and encouragement for efforts made. Your child needs that in order to develop a positive self-image. It's important that young children experience the satisfaction of knowing they are doing things "right." That more than anything else stimulates the confidence needed for developing a capacity for independent action.

Some parents consistently underestimate the importance of positive reinforcement. They focus on behavior that must be corrected. They don't provide recognition for their child's measuring up to expectations. They see nothing remarkable in that. Why reward a child for doing what he or she is supposed to do?

The child, however, may perceive this as a kind of negative approach to things and will respond accordingly. For example he or she learns that one behaves according to rules or expectations primarily to avoid punishment or disapproval. There's no sense of payoff for doing things right, except in the sense that escaping punishment or disapproval provides relief from the constant threat of being rated unsatisfactory or deficient. That provides a very poor orientation for eventually learning to deal with decision situations. Instead of the child's looking to achieve positive goals, it's very likely he or she will come to approach decisions with an eye toward avoiding negative consequences. And that, as we've seen already, is a far cry from learning to assess situations so as to achieve the best results possible.

Provide your child regular positive reinforcement. Let him or her know from the outset that all efforts at accomplishment will win favor. Don't focus your attention primarily on correcting problem situations.

### Consistency

It's also important that you display consistency in your responses to your child's behavior. It's through seeing that certain consequences consistently relate to certain behaviors that your child is prompted into a responsible pattern of behavior. That's how he or she learns that what happens as the result of a choice of action is predictable. Inconsistency makes it impossible for the child to know what to expect.

Parents of very young children often contribute to confusion here. On one occasion they will label a behavior "cute" and show themselves amused by it, then they'll demonstrate impatient annoyance when it is repeated. You can hardly blame the child for getting confused and insecure. The first response seemed to indicate approval, while the second clearly indicated the opposite.

You can't reasonably expect your child to develop a pattern of behavior that's consistent if you are inconsistent in your cues on what is or isn't acceptable.

It's in establishing and maintaining routines that you develop the setting for consistent behavior, on both your part and your child's. It's in the repetition that routines provide that your preschool child comes to recognize what is expected on a day-to-day basis. Meals, play time, baths, bedtime, etc., all provide daily opportunities for reinforcing an awareness of behavioral expectations. Each presents a familiar set of circumstances in which the young child naturally learns something about what's involved in making decisions. At first it will be mostly a matter of following directions and associating parental reactions with how those are followed. Gradually you'll find your child's sense of consequences begins to extend beyond just your reactions. Instead of only looking for approval or trying to avoid disapproval, your child comes to see that there are further consequences he or she can select.

Take, for example, the common situation of the young child learning to eat without assistance. In the early stages of this process, it's parental direction and encouragement that prompt progress here. Your child picks up a spoon and tries to eat as an imitative gesture or in response to your coaching. The consequences at first are all parent-associated; there's no immediate connection drawn between using the spoon and satisfying one's appetite. However, as the child grows more proficient in the use of eating utensils, he or she learns it has a consequence relating to something beyond parental favor. Eventually the child sees that satisfying hunger depends on the willingness to feed himself or herself. Self-feeding is no longer just a way of winning parental approval.

## The Intermediate Nature of Approval

When it comes to recognizing consequences, parental approval functions best as something of an intermediate goal. Very young children are naturally motivated to seek parental approval. That's why an attitude of positive response to your child's efforts at achievement is so very important. It provides the immediate reinforcement your child is looking for.

But there is a trap to beware of here. Ultimately, your objective should *not* be to establish your approval as the primary consequence to be sought after. Your efforts should aim at getting your child to recognize that a world of consequences exists beyond your approval. Granted, your approval remains a factor in your child's behavior until he or she matures into full independence. But you want your approval to prime your child for recognition of the objective consequences to consider when deciding on an action, not to be the end in itself. Otherwise your child is pushed into always reaching for your solutions to his or her situations, with the object being to win your approval rather than to respond to the challenge of the situation.

To prepare your child for eventual mature independence, use your approval to point to an objective benefit the child will experience in a situation. Don't set it up as the primary goal to be worked for.

While your preschool child is obviously years away from achieving independence, the habits you develop in guiding and responding to his or her behavior now can significantly influence later development.

Joyce had recently received a pair of shiny new black shoes of which she was very proud. She wore them to nursery school the first two days she had them. On the third day, because it was raining and muddy outside, her mother told her to wear her old brown shoes. Joyce nevertheless came downstairs wearing the new pair. Seeing this, her mother became very cross, telling Joyce that she was a bad girl not to have minded mother's instructions and that mother would put away her new shoes altogether if Joyce did not learn to mind what she'd been told. Joyce tearfully retreated up the stairs to change her shoes.

Here's a clear-cut case of a parent stressing compliance with instructions so as to emphasize the primary importance of approval. The child's behavior is characterized in judgmental terms—Joyce is "a bad girl"—and corrective direction is backed up by the threat of negative consequences related to the "bad" behavior. Joyce obviously goes back up the stairs prompted by a fear of what will happen unless mother's disapproval is somehow abated. Her mother probably feels she handled the situation well. After all, Joyce has gone back up to change her shoes, and now the new pair won't be ruined.

But let's look at this situation in terms of the consequences involved. Joyce's mother is motivated by an awareness that wearing the new shoes this day subjects them to the threat of possible ruin. So in her mind, Joyce's decision to put on the shoes is a poor one. Ruined shoes is a consequence to be avoided. However, Joyce has probably not made a connection between her decision to wear her new shoes and the likely consequence—that such a decision today subjects them to the risk of ruin. She is thinking only of the pride she feels in wearing them to school.

When her mother subsequently scolds and threatens her for "not minding," the sense of consequences Joyce develops comes to revolve around the fact that she has displeased her mother. Her aim in correcting her decision is to avert the threatened consequences arising from her mother's displeasure. She does not come to the awareness that consequences are involved that she herself would prefer to avoid, regardless of anyone else's view of the circumstances. And nothing her mother has done has helped her make that connection.

Parents who fall into the all-too-common habit of expressing reactions to their children's behavior primarily in terms of "good" or "bad," or "right" or "wrong," miss daily opportunities to help their child make a connection between actions and direct consequences that influence the child regardless of parental feelings. It's particularly important in the preschool years that one sees parents settle on this approach. Preschool children are still so dependent that they respond to the behavior cues given in these terms. The problem is that the parents, without realizing it, program their child into a pattern of *responsive* behavior that emphasizes pleasing others. The groundwork for developing *responsible* behavior, which requires that the child see a more direct connection between his or her actions and what develops as a result, is not firmly laid.

### Recognizing Individuality

Parents who set the emphasis on "being a good boy/girl" also tend to overlook needs the child may have as an individual. Without realizing it, they set up their expectations as the point of main focus. Then, when the child's behavior is at odds with those expectations, they tend to concentrate on pulling it back into line. They don't think to ask what the child may be trying to express in terms of needs he or she feels.

> Sam's parents noticed that he always seemed fresh and ill behaved when his older sister returned from prep school during the holidays. This pattern repeated itself over the course of the year, and they were really upset with it. They scolded Sam for his behavior each time, telling him this was not how they expected him to behave, but things did not improve. The situation became upsetting for the entire family.

In this case, the parents' initial reaction was clearly not enough to prompt change in their child's behavior. Something was evidently troubling Sam that would not be relieved by his conforming to his parents' expectations.

Fortunately, Sam's parents finally recognized that some difficulty he was experiencing must lie at the root of his unsettling behavior. They sat down with him and talked with him to find out what the problem was. They soon discovered that Sam felt left out during vacation times because all the attention seemed to focus on his older sister and baby brother.

Once they discovered that he was feeling left out, Sam's parents were careful to refocus some of their attention during vacation times so that he, too, felt drawn into family discussions and activities. They prompted him to share his accomplishments with his sister, so that he, too, looked forward to her visits from school. Sam's father also decided he would do something with Sam during holiday times so that Sam would get additional attention in a positive fashion. Sam soon found he had things to tell about and share during vacation time, and this quickly removed his sense of being the overlooked member of the family on these occasions.

Children's behavior is purposeful as a rule. They may not have drawn clear connections between what they do and what they get, but what they do generally has an aim, even if they may not be able to state that clearly. In Sam's case, his misbehavior clearly aimed at winning himself a measure of the attention he felt he was being denied. Even though that attention was expressed in disapproving terms—he was scolded for his bad manners—the fact is he got it. While he almost certainly would have no concept of goal priorities, he instinctively felt gaining some kind of attention during these periods was more important than winning quiet approval. On a very basic level, Sam was asserting his individuality, expressing his particular sense of need. Had his parents taken the attitude that the thing to concentrate on was getting him to conform to their expectations, without making an effort to assess his needs, the pattern would have been set for a protracted conflict situation.

The thought may occur to you that this could set you up for a kind of juvenile blackmail. Should you give in to your child's every demand for attention to indicate your respect for his or her individuality?

Of course not. Sometimes you will have to impose limits on your child's demands for attention. Recognize, however, that this is something quite different from ignoring your child's demands altogether. Be attentive to behavior at all times.

When a pattern of behavior develops that proves disruptive or troublesome, look at what is happening. It may very well be that responding with the kind of attention the child is demanding immediately would be counterproductive. The result could be to encourage similar behavior subsequently. But some adjustment will be called for. Examine the situation so that the adjustment you try to implement considers all the pertinent factors. Don't settle for "cosmetic" improvements that fail to take an underlying difficulty on the child's part into account.

## SETTING LIMITS ON YOUNG CHILDREN

So how do you go about getting your child to behave without fracturing his or her sensitive individuality? How do you use your approval constructively, without that turning into a double-edged sword that cuts away his or her sense of self? It hardly seems you can do anything and not run the risk of permanently damaging a tender psyche.

Certainly the danger exists that misplaced emphasis in your approach to your young child's behavior can compromise his or her later growth into independent maturity. That's why it's important you consciously apply positive principles to your functioning as a parent.

But don't panic that any little error on your part inevitably harms your child's potential for capable self-expression in later years. Young children are very impressionable, it's true. But they are also very resilient. They can take a great many things in stride, as long as they're not habitually exposed to erratic behavior on your part, or to behavior that continually subordinates their needs to your personal priorities and expectations.

A child may well become confused and frightened if you lash out in anger at some quite ordinary behavior that you cannot tolerate for a moment. But as long as you've established a general routine within which he or she continues to experience a positive, caring attitude from you, that confusion and fright will dissipate. The flow you establish through your regular routine will provide the necessary reassurance that you care. The evidence that you as a rule are concerned with his or her needs and feelings will hold in check whatever insecurity might have surfaced as a result of your momentary inability to cope with his or her behavior.

### Consider Basic Needs

When it comes to setting or enforcing limits on your child's behavior, always consider the child's basic needs. We're not talking here of needs the child may think to have in the moment, although somewhere those have to be taken into account. We're talking of needs fundamental to the development of a personality able to cope with the many demands and opportunities of the world at large while feeling a secure sense of place within that world. A child's momentary need for attention may best be put off. But the basic needs—for security, love, and self-expression—should be weighed and reviewed whenever it comes to defining limits on behavior and imposing consequences.

How do you know whether your general pattern in setting behavioral limits adequately takes basic needs into account? Well, in setting limits remember that the idea is to make the child feel worthwhile, to encourage self-expression, to promote learning from past mistakes, and to establish good communication between you and your child.

Rate yourself in the areas indicated below. Each of the listed parental reactions promotes your child's positive experience of self and encourages development of the capability for making good decisions.

| Do you: | Often | Seldom | Never |
|---|---|---|---|
| Show real affection for your child? | _____ | _____ | _____ |
| Let your child vent feelings? | _____ | _____ | _____ |
| Explain your moods to your child? | _____ | _____ | _____ |
| Check your expectations for realism? | _____ | _____ | _____ |
| Allow for failure? | _____ | _____ | _____ |
| Provide special times where your child can discuss things with you? | _____ | _____ | _____ |
| Give praise for big *and* little things? | _____ | _____ | _____ |
| Balance criticisms in the context of strengths? | _____ | _____ | _____ |

A large number of *seldoms* or *nevers* in these areas indicates a probability that you've set limits without due regard to your child's basic needs. You may well be setting yourself up as an ultimate authority figure—someone to be heeded at all times, someone who is not to be questioned. That may be a convenient way to keep control of your preschool child, but it sets the scene for a lack of communication in later years. Your child will be inclined to move in one of two directions: an eventual resentful rebellion aimed at "self-liberation," but without the developed capacity for managing personal affairs to best effect; or "caved-in" acquiescence to the dictates of others around him or her, with low self-esteem and no sense of being able to manage personal affairs with any competence.

Authoritarian parents fail to recognize that their parenting techniques implicitly establish the child as a second-class identity. And that is at the root of many problems arising with their children in later years.

But an authoritarian failure to take the child's needs into account isn't the only source of difficulty. You may have ranked yourself fairly high in the areas listed above and still hurt your child's chance of emerging a self-confident, practical decisionmaker. Your difficulty may be that you take a permissive approach that is counterproductive. You may be one of those parents who so emphasizes "making nice" with your child that you effectively minimize the learning experience that consequences provide. You demonstrate too much concern to satisfy your child's wants, confusing those with needs.

Parents who are too quick to interpose themselves between the child and any consequences growing out of his or her actions do the child a disservice. On a social level, the child may come to believe that anything goes; there will always be someone to clean up after him or her. And a dangerous sense of invulnerability may characterize the child's approach to the experience of reality. The child grows up in something of a fools' paradise, and the parents set themselves the task of making that seem real.

Also, in the absence of clear consequences established through imposing and enforcing limits, there's no way to sort out family priorities systematically. There's no standard for resolving conflict. In extreme cases permissive parents get around that dilemma by giving priority to the child's wants whenever there's any hint of conflict. That, however, tends to foster expectations in the child that he or she properly has center stage at all times. There's no encouragement to respect others. You may eventually find the situation something like that depicted in the Joan Crawford movie classic *Mildred Pierce*.

There are long-term consequences of your approach to your child's needs now. However, don't overlook the short-term benefits. Take care to address your child's basic needs attentively, and you move toward immediate positive consequences—a well-adjusted child secure in a caring home environment—without needing to fear the probability of turning out an adult who is poorly prepared to take positive control of his or her own life at maturity.

### Some Guidelines for Setting Limits

As the parent of a preschool child, you are charged with total responsibility in almost every area. You're not there simply to attend to emotional needs; you also have to attend to your child's health and safety. You can't concentrate only on developing your child's sense of individuality and self-worth; you also have to provide a realistic orientation to the world.

Some parents find the double focus—on the ideal and the real—difficult to balance. They'd like to encourage self-expression, but they fear that may expose the child to physical danger. They want the child to grow up in an atmosphere of love and security, but they see a need to head off any illusion that the world reflects that kind of environment. How do you encourage your child to reach for the stars when reality imposes so many limits on what's likely or possible? Don't you have to protect your child from running head-on into the limits that reality imposes?

Yes and no. Your child does need special attention and protection during the first years of life. But the point should not be to insulate him or her from reality. Your child must come to recognize that the world in which we all live exerts its own influence. Without this recognition, he or she will not be able to function well in it. There is no chance to reach the stars without a firm launching pad from which to start.

Your limits should not be set to keep your child from suffering any of the pains and frustrations imposed by reality. Your limits should be devised *to help your child cope* with the inevitable demands of reality, however uncomfortable some of those may prove.

*Allow your child the experience of natural consequences to behavior.* It's in learning that certain effects naturally attach to certain actions that children come to understand that consequences are a consideration in every behavior. Allowing your child to suffer the frustrations and discomfort that naturally result from certain actions provides the foundation for making realistic judgments about actions. You have to be judicious, of course. It would be dangerous and cruel to let your child burn himself or herself just to learn to be careful with things that are hot. The lessons of pain are learned soon enough in the course of everyday life.

But there are many actions young children freely indulge in that do not expose them to danger while subjecting them to natural consequences. Your allowing your child to experience those without interposing yourself to make things immediately "better" helps your child more quickly see the connection between action and outcome. Three-year-old Jeremy, who loses every new ball within an hour or two of receiving it, is best taught through the experience of natural consequences— carelessness results in loss of the ball—that his actions affect his subsequent situation: Jeremy will have no ball to play with. If the too-concerned parent feeds him a constant supply of new balls, Jeremy will be that much slower to make the connection between careless actions and the risk of loss.

In allowing your child to learn from the natural consequences of his or her own actions, you help your child see that he or she plays a deciding role in what happens to him or her. By refusing to assume the burden of protecting your child from all unpleasant outcomes that result from his or her behavior, you take the first step toward prompting a sense of responsibility.

Does that mean you should display indifference when your child suffers a natural consequence he or she finds distressing? Not at all. It is perfectly appropriate to demonstrate a caring interest. However, it's best to allow your child's discomfort—as long as that is not potentially injurious or traumatic over the long run—to make its own impression. Don't run to immediately provide remedy from that. You can show sympathy, but let the lesson be learned: Carelessness easily results in the child's losing something he or she finds enjoyable.

If, within boundaries set by a concern for your child's health and safety and those of others who may be affected, you allow natural consequences to have their own effect, your child won't mistakenly conclude that limits are all a matter of parental influence. Trying to control the effect natural consequences have will make it appear that the limits set by reality are all under your control. You may in fact encourage carelessness through trying to protect your child from the consequences of carelessness.

An overprotective pattern can have serious long-term effects. Look around you in society today, and you will see many teenagers and young adults still turning expectantly to their parents to shield them from the uncomfortable results of their own lack of good judgment. Never having had to suffer the natural consequences of their poorly chosen actions, they never learned to take responsibility for themselves. They never understood the difference between doing something on impulse and doing something in the carrying out of a good decision.

*See the establishment of limits as a decision to be made.* You can't leave it at natural consequences. There are also the priorities in the family philosophy to take into account. There's a social order your child has to be prepared for.

Follow the process set out in Part One of this book for determining limits governing behavior. Your family philosophy will help you here. Ask yourself: What are the values that I wish to emphasize? What are the goals my limits will aim at? What's the range of alternatives in any case? What do I need to know in order to evaluate those? What likely outcomes attach to the imposition and enforcement of limits I'm considering?

It's a sad fact that most families fail to consciously consider long-range objectives in setting limits on behavior. They take a short-term approach, making decisions purely on an ad hoc (as the situation arises) basis. That introduces several potential problems. One is a likely emphasis on winning compliance in the situation at hand without considering whether the child understands what's happening. The parents, assuming compliance is the issue, consider everything to be in order once an on-the-spot directive is obeyed. They don't think to review whether the child has understood anything about the directive—what it aims at, if/that his or her needs as an individual are being taken into account.

Setting limits only as situations arise also tends to keep things in something of a state of confusion. The child has no grounds for anticipating reaction to certain behaviors. When the reaction comes, and with it whatever consequences the parents then and there decide to impose, the child experiences frightened bewilderment. What happened? What suddenly made everything go sour?

Of course you can't anticipate everything. Sometimes you have to act quickly in response to an unexpected situation or development.

Yes, but there's a difference in general style and follow-up. An attentive, caring parent builds a framework wherein the child comes to recognize likely consequences for limits that assume a familiar dimension. Most limits and consequences fit into that framework. When an unexpected situation requires immediate discipline—imposing and enforcing a new limit—the parent takes the child's subsequent bewilderment into account. There's a caring response to that at the same time the limit is enforced.

Because with very young children the ability to make a connection between action and consequence is still developing, some reassurance is called for when unfamiliar limits come into play. Otherwise, in suddenly imposing a new consequence, you come across like Dr. Jekyll just turned into Mr. Hyde. The child may have no idea what set you off.

If you leave it at an angry reprimand or scolding, Mr. Hyde is who you leave it as. Now all the child knows is that at certain unpredictable moments you flash into an ominous temperament. Reassure him or her that you haven't taken on a new personality. Draw the connection between action and discipline. Do that in simple terms. No, the child may still not understand your explanation. However, he or she will sense that you care. Within time, perhaps a very brief time, your child will pick up on the connection.

Parents who make a habit of ad hoc discipline provide the child no clear sense of pattern about acceptable behavior. They are also more likely to apply the criterion of convenience, which means something may be all right one time—at least tolerated—and the next time prove unacceptable. That boils down to inconsistency and all the problems inconsistency gives rise to.

Treat the establishment of limits as a decision. Then your disciplinary actions can work together toward clearly established goals that take interests on all sides into account. And your disciplinary actions will provide your child an orientation to the connection between choice and consequence. The child will see an order to life. The child will see that his or her behavior influences that order.

*Make limits clear enough so that the child understands when behavior becomes unacceptable.* For the very young child, that means setting things in terms that are kept simple. It will take time even for simple limits to be understood; qualifying them right away only complicates the child's efforts at understanding. For example, telling four-year-old Anthony it's all right to throw rocks but not in the direction of other children gives both a *yes* and a *no* message. Anthony may hear one and not the other. Or he may observe the limit as he understands it, but his sense of direction may be too close for you or for another parent.

*Consider the child's self-esteem in setting limits.* Your aim is to help your child, not just to discourage unacceptable behavior. Don't articulate limits so as to belittle him or her. Don't aim them as if in remedy for his or her inabilities or failures.

It's best to state limits in impersonal terms as much as possible. Toys are not for throwing. Shouting at others is not permitted. Using other people's things without permission is not allowed. Bedtime is right after storytime. In this way a more general sense of limits emerges. While some limits—bedtime, for example—will apply specifically to the child, others will tie in to the overall family code of behavior. Expressing limits you want the child to observe in impersonal terms will enable him or her more readily to see them as fitting into a framework that applies to the whole family.

*Formulate limits in specific terms.* Don't set them in terms that are so general they can mean almost anything.

A lot of parents set limits phrased along the lines of "You have to be a good girl when company's here" or "You have to behave yourself when you're out with Mommy shopping." Yes, some vague sense of what it means to be "a good girl" or "to behave" will eventually emerge. It's easier and more to the point to set limits in terms of specific actions: "We play quietly when company's here"; "pulling packages off the supermarket shelf is not permitted." That way the child knows precisely what action to follow or avoid in the situation at hand.

*Establish clear consequences for violating limits. Tailor them to fit the circumstance as closely as possible.* The limits you set have no meaning if you do not enforce them. The way you enforce them is to establish a consequence that pulls the child back within limits.

Consequences in this area rarely prove enjoyable for the child. And some parents find they haven't the heart to impose discipline that a small child will find unpleasant or upsetting, even though they'd prefer that the child stay within behavioral limits he or she keeps testing. But unless limits are enforced, you relinquish control over your child's behavior. You handicap the child in drawing connections between behavior choices and consequences. You set up a situation where limits can easily be disregarded, where respect for the family order fails to develop.

When it comes to deciding what consequences to establish, recognize that the more specifically they relate to the activity and setting at hand, the more readily behavior in that activity/ setting is brought under control. The more immediate their application, the more quickly the child makes the connection between choice of behavior and the consequence it leads to. In either situation above, parents often respond with anger at a behavior and then promise to mete out the consequence later. And the consequence may be the same consequence that applies for other infractions of limits set, e.g., a spanking.

Your son Benjamin is noisy and/or continually whines for attention while you are visiting with a friend. Instead of angry threats and delayed consequences that apply in a dozen situations, establish and enforce a consequence tailored to the circumstances. If Benjamin will not heed the limit "We play quietly when company's here," establish as the consequence removing and safely confining him to another room of the house until your visitor has gone.

Amy, your three-year-old, continually reaches for and pulls packages off the supermarket shelf while you are out shopping with her. Make it clear you will restrain her freedom of movement unless she abides by the limit set in this circumstance. Or, if this is feasible, refuse Amy further trips with you to the supermarket until she demonstrates control.

That brings us to a next rule of thumb in setting limits.

*Establish positive as well as negative consequences in connection with limits on behavior.* Many parents think of consequences only in terms of restricting and controlling behavior. They see consequences as negatives that work out to a series of "Don't . . . or else" guidelines and little more.

Think of limits as guidelines for achievement as well as for controlling misbehavior. Award reinforcing recognition when your child is alert to limits that have been established.

Young children typically seek to prove themselves able to take on new responsibility. They are easily discouraged if the limits set on them do not make any allowance for progress toward maturity. A child who feels he or she is ready to take on an additional responsibility will be resentful if limits are imposed that block him or her there. That resentment often surfaces in complaints about being treated like a baby. Or it can surface in misbehavior that you may not so immediately connect with frustration at not receiving recognition for greater maturity.

Many of Kim's friends attended the same day care program, and since they were from the same apartment building, they all gathered and walked to the day care center, which was nearby. Kim, however, was not allowed to do this, because her mother was concerned for her safety. It was apparent that something bothered Kim each morning when her mother walked her to the center. Kim waited until the last minute to get ready, resulting in her regularly being late arriving. Her mother was very irritated by the situation and several times had to drag her out of the house physically. Kim complained she was being treated like a baby. Her mother's reply was that she was acting like a baby and didn't show enough maturity to go to the center on her own.

Kim's mother has set and enforced limits that do not take into account her daughter's gradual move to greater maturity. This may very well diminish Kim's chances of learning to be more independent. Her mother's concern for safety, while probably warranted, could be satisfied by exploring alternatives that recognize Kim's achievements in the area of going short distances without getting lost or distracted from her destination. One solution might be as simple as letting Kim go to school with her friends after her mother has observed the process over a trial period. It might be appropriate to discuss concerns with other parents as well.

Note that establishing positive consequences for abiding by limits, as opposed to concentrating just on negative consequences, has a further benefit. It tends to generate a more accepting attitude in the child, who comes to see that limits are also standards for measuring progress. They are not just a series of barriers imposed on independent behavior.

*Take the child's uniqueness into account in setting limits.* Children progress at different rates, and it's all too easy to draw comparisons between them that do nothing to encourage good behavior or to prompt greater achievement.

> Kevin came home from nursery school with a report from his teacher that was not especially good. His mother quickly showed her disappointment by telling him his older sister had done much better. She also told him he would have to practice school activities more and would not be able to watch as much television.

This kind of response does not take into account what is happening with the child. The parent is applying a standard of achievement set by another child without pausing to consider possible differences in the situation or the child's abilities, feelings, or needs. Her reaction may well have the effect of lowering Kevin's self-esteem and discouraging him from maintaining what effort he has been making.

With respect to teaching her child about limits, Kevin's mother is not tying behavior directly to consequences. She has not identified where Kevin has failed to abide by limits, nor imposed a consequence related to that failure. The message to Kevin is that parental approval depends on his duplicating his sister's achievements. Never mind that he and his sister are two different individuals, each with their own unique qualities and needs. Failing to link the consequence imposed with behavioral limits Kevin knows apply to him, his mother has also given a signal that limits do not provide reliable behavioral guidelines. That can lead to limits subsequently being discounted in favor of imitative behavior based on inappropriate standards for the child.

*Recognize that limits do have to be adjusted from time to time.* The general guidelines for determining when adjustments are timely or necessary have been given in Chapter 10. With preschool children the point to remember is that adjustments have to take into account their developing capability for independent action in certain areas, while continuing to recognize that they have only limited experience in the ways and dangers of the world at large. As a parent, you have to strive for a balance.

So how will you know whether the limits you've set work toward the goal of preparing your child for eventual independent maturity? (It may seem odd to contemplate that eventuality when your child is no more than three or four years old, but these are crucial years. They set patterns you will tend to follow through the next decade and a half. For your child, they set patterns that will exert their influence over a lifetime.)

To rate your framework of limits, see if you can answer yes to each of the following questions:

- Are limits clear enough so that your child understands when behavior becomes unacceptable?

- Do they take your child's individuality into account, allowing him or her to feel comfortable with his or her own uniqueness?
- Are they enforced so that the child continues to sense your affection and love even after a mistake has been made?
- Do they encourage a healthy willingness to try new things?
- Do they include the important element of recognition for achievement, so the child can experience a sense of growing competence?

If your answer to any of these questions is no, it may be that the way you've set and applied limits to some degree discourages development of abilities and attitudes that go into making good decisions.

### CAN YOU EXPECT YOUR PRESCHOOL CHILD TO UNDERSTAND LIMITS?

You can't reasonably expect an infant to understand limits and why they are necessary or desirable. However, you will start setting limits when your child is still an infant.

Even before your child is a year old, you will be developing routines. You'll show a pattern of response to various behaviors—for example, to your child's demands for attention. If you are consistent in the pattern you set, your child will begin to recognize it and respond accordingly, even though he or she won't actually understand why you behave as you do.

Your routines will include distinct elements of limitation. They will probably also include elements of encouragement to which your child will react. Your careful attention to routines you establish does much to prime your child for a gradual recognition of what is expected of him or her in terms of acceptable behavior, and what is permitted or encouraged in terms of exploring the world at large.

Even though at this early age you may feel it's premature to work out a framework for governing your child's behavior, it's a good idea to do just that. And in doing so, pay as much attention to the kind of behavior you wish to encourage as you would with an older child. Be clear in your mind what your values and goals are. And, most important, be aware that even your infant child has basic needs in the areas of love, security, and self-expression. Failure to take those into account from the very start will lead to difficulties from the start when it comes to fostering good behavior.

I particularly encourage parents of young children to begin right away to develop a habit of articulating the rationale behind limits set and consequences applied to behavior. It's an excellent consciousness-raising technique for the parent—it gives you a clearer sense of what you're doing and why. It ensures that the child will, as soon as possible, begin to draw elementary connections between actions and consequences.

Most parents don't think to do this. They see no point to it, as the child is too young to comprehend what is happening. That will be true for a time, of course. But if you wait to take a more conscious, explicit approach until you deem the child ready, you risk developing a habit of setting and enforcing limits without a clearly thought-out, explainable rationale. By the time your child can begin responding on a more aware level, your routine may already be so habitual that you miss opportunities for helpful guidance in the early years. You may think you can wait until your child is three years old before making an effort to explain limits and consequences to him or her. However, in doing so, you risk that your imposing limits without explanation may become so habitual that you don't remember when the time comes to make your planned adjustment.

Starting early, even before the child can catch on to much if anything of what's going on, ensures you're already providing positive input the moment he or she starts making conscious connections about behavior. And you won't find yourself struggling to break habits that don't take your child's need to understand into account.

No, you can't expect very young children to understand what limits are all about. But you will find they come to recognize those that are established through consistent routine relatively early on. You will see them begin to respond to the pattern of limits you've established as these are applied. If you take care to develop a pattern that is clear, if you make consistent effort to draw the connection between behavior and consequences that the child experiences, you will find yourself achieving an immediate goal—a well-adjusted child secure in a caring home environment—that leads toward a long-range objective: an individual primed to take responsible control over the life decisions facing him or her.

# 12

# Helping with Your Child's
# First Decisions

The father reached for three-year-old Sarah's tiny hand and held it firmly as they approached the curb. At the curb they stopped, and the father demonstrated how to look both ways and what to look for with regard to approaching cars.

Sarah imitated her father perfectly, and when the way was clear, they crossed the street together briskly. Once on the other side, they stopped, turned around, and recrossed the street after carefully looking both ways for oncoming traffic.

After doing this five or six times, the two crossed the street without the father holding Sarah's hand. Then, once the father was satisfied that the procedure had been mastered and was being carefully followed, he allowed Sarah to cross to the other side of the street and return again without accompaniment. It was easy to see that both father and Sarah were very proud of this accomplishment.

This little scenario illustrates almost perfectly what's involved in helping very young children with their first decisions. First you lead them by the hand, introducing them to routines that are new to them, ensuring they follow in the direction you want them to go. Then you practice the routine with them, to make sure they become fully familiar with it. And once they seem to have mastered it, you step back to let them try it on their own. Meanwhile, you keep a watchful eye for unexpected developments and errors in judgment that may introduce difficulties a young child is not yet able to understand or handle.

You may not see this approach to routines as providing your child any sense of what decisions are and how they are made. Nevertheless, it does.

Consider for a moment what's involved here. On a very elemental level, this scenario includes all of the steps that go into reaching decisions:

- There's an initial *value* identified and stressed—safety.
- There's an immediate *goal*—getting across the street.
- There are *alternatives*—to go immediately, to wait, or even not to go at all.
- There's an *information* search—looking to see whether traffic is coming and noting how oncoming cars are behaving.
- There's a sense of *consequences*—for the child probably limited to demonstrating achievement and winning parental approval; for the parent undoubtedly focused on safely arriving on the other side of the street whenever it comes to the child crossing the street.
- There's *action*—the actual movement across the street.
- There's *review* of the decision made—parent and child recognize an achievement that contributes to the child's ability to act more independently in a responsible fashion.

Providing children guidance is very much a matter of making decisions. Because this is so, virtually every parental action presents an opportunity for teaching something about decisions.

In the preceding chapter we've already noted the importance of patterns you establish in your child's first years of life. Well, your approach in introducing him or her to the ordinary routines of life establishes a particularly influential pattern. If you conscientiously follow the framework previously introduced for reaching well-considered decisions, from the very beginning you'll orient your child to that as a natural process to follow.

Establishing routines for your child amounts to pointing him or her in the right direction to be taken in deciding what to do or not to do in given situations. Your child almost certainly won't realize all the implications involved. It's not essential that he or she does. When you get right down to it, right now your child can't.

Look back to the little scenario at the opening of this chapter. Is it likely Sarah understands the importance of crossing the street safely? Probably not. Safety is an abstraction that can't mean much to her. Sarah's sense of consequences almost certainly fails to include the risk of being injured or killed by an oncoming car, although some instinct for self-preservation may come into play if ever she's actually in danger of being run over.

But as a parent, you don't want to trust to a possible instinct for self-preservation in this situation. You don't want your child suddenly faced with the necessity of scrambling for his or her life. Regardless of whether or nor your child comprehends what safety is all about, it is vital to develop and practice a habit of safety. For the time being, it's all right if your child's sense of consequences relates more to your approval than to risk of injury or death—as long as the habit that can keep him or her safe comes into play each time it is necessary to cross the street. Crossing the street amounts to a decision, even though he or she may not understand it as such.

### BUILDING ROUTINES

As soon as your child is old enough to do—that is, to act in a given circumstance—he or she is old enough to begin learning to decide.

You will have to lead your child by the hand through his or her first decisions. You will have to build routine into everyday behavior, so that the response to regularly encountered situations predictably leads to desirable outcomes, whether or not they are consciously recognized as such. You want your child to develop a habit of response that entails recognizing choices and looking for information before jumping into action.

Initially, this all happens on a very rudimentary level. The alternatives may only be yes or no—to cross the street or to wait, to eat hot cereal now or to let it cool first. The information check may take only one consideration into account— whether traffic is approaching from either side, whether a cautious first taste indicates the cereal is cool enough to eat comfortably.

Even on this simple level, you can get your child to begin following the decisionmaking framework. The earlier that is incorporated into the daily routine, the sooner your child will be ready to apply it on a more conscious level to new situations.

The routines of childhood include activities and concerns that carry through a lifetime. Psychologists and psychiatrists unanimously agree that patterns of behavior established in the first five years of childhood exert profound influence throughout life.

Think about the routines you are establishing with your child. Be careful to ensure they have a clearly constructive focus and effect. Otherwise you risk your child's developing habits that may trouble him or her for years to come.

Make a list of the routines. What they are in specific will differ from family to family, but they will relate primarily to the following areas:

- Mealtimes and eating behavior
- Bedtime
- Getting dressed
- Toilet and sanitary habits
- Attentiveness to parental direction

- Respect for property
- Social behavior

Once you've drawn up your inventory of routines, approach each one as a decision. Ask yourself these questions.

1. What **values** does the routine promote?
2. What specific *goal* does it aim for?
3. What *alternatives* have you considered?
4. What *information* are you relying on?
5. What *consequences* are involved?
6. What is the *action* to be taken?
7. In *review,* is the routine working constructively?

Once you've taken the time to consider routines this way, you'll have a good understanding of where each provides a benefit. You'll see more clearly why you've chosen to follow a set way of doing things; you'll know why alternative approaches aren't satisfactory. Or, you may discover there's a better way you didn't see before.

With any routine, make a point of identifying what the benefit is to your child. After all, you want him or her to follow it, to adopt it as his or her own. If it is to have a constructive effect on your child, it must somehow take his or her interests into account.

Of course, routines aren't established only for the benefit of the children. Many also serve to provide the parents' lives a certain order. For example, you may establish a routine that provides either parent a quiet "do not disturb" time alone. You want your child to observe the routine, but the benefit you look toward is primarily yours.

It's not necessary, however, that the child be the primary focus of benefit in every family routine. That's impossible. But in all routines, including those that aim at providing the parents primary benefit, there should be a regard for the effect on the child. There will always be an effect, and you want it to contribute to your child's developing abilities, not to stifle those.

Millie's mother enjoyed the company of a neighborhood friend who frequently dropped in during the midafternoon. Because she wanted to be free of any distractions Millie might otherwise provide, she established the routine of putting Millie to bed every time the friend was to stop by for a visit. Millie's frequent protests and tears only hardened her mother's determination to have her out of the way while the friend visited.

Here's a case where a routine exists only for the parent's convenience. The child is literally put to the side and out of mind so the parent can enjoy time off to herself. Nothing in this routine contributes to Millie's learning behavior that expands her ability to relate to the world around her. She's being treated like an object, not like a person. That's a very poor perspective from which to develop a capacity for making decisions.

Timothy looked forward to his father's return from work each day. Upon hearing him come into the house, he'd race to greet him, shouting loudly and demanding his father's immediate attention. After a time, his father decided he preferred a simpler greeting, followed by a quiet half hour in which he could relax from the pressures of work. In establishing this new routine, Timothy's parents explained that Daddy needed time to rest when he came home from work. Timothy was to play quietly during that time. Daddy would then spend special time with him after supper.

In this case, too, the routine established works primarily for the parent's benefit. But note that it also takes the child into consideration as a person with interests at stake. That's the key. It may still take Timothy a while to adjust to the change, but he will see that his interests have been taken into account. Because a sense of benefit attaches to the routine for him, too, in the long run he will find it easy to accept. In the process, he'll have learned a valuable lesson about others' needs requiring his consideration.

### Explaining Why

The routines you establish with your child will inevitably influence how he or she views the world at large. Built into your child's repertory of standard behaviors, they will provide an experience base he or she unconsciously refers to whenever deciding to act.

But remember, you want to go beyond just programming your child into constructive behavior. You want your child to develop an ability to make *conscious* choices well. That takes in more than automatically following routines you have established with his or her benefit and interests in mind. That includes your child's own reflection on what will serve his or her interests best. It means a consideration of alternatives.

While it will still be a few years before your child can understand decisionmaking as a process, the way you approach establishing routines can result in his or her beginning to employ the process early on. All it takes is your following the decision framework and prompting your child into a gradual recognition of it as a natural process to follow.

But you must be careful to explain everything with the child's perspective and interests in mind. That's the only way to make the process natural to him or her.

You'll be helped here by your child's own natural curiosity. By the age of two to three years, *why* will have become a prominent word in his or her vocabulary. If you've followed the decision framework in establishing routines, you'll have answers to some very important *why* questions. You'll be set to help your child begin to make conscious connections about behavior choices and consequences. No, your child may not understand everything right away, but he or she will sense an order to things. Your child will start to look for the pattern. Eventually he or she will recognize it.

You don't have to label the process elements. That involves

abstractions beyond your child's comprehension. Just be sure they are all in place. Keep the explanations themselves as simple as possible. Start with the connections your child can make.

> John was being taught to wash his hands before every meal. His mother patiently showed him how to wet his hands, lather up with soap, then rinse off and dry. When John asked why he had to wash hands before eating, his mother explained that it was so his hands would be really clean. Dirty hands sometimes carried germs that could make him sick. By washing his hands before meals, he was washing off germs that otherwise he might eat with his food.

In this example, the parent provides information the child can use to begin making sense out of what he is being required to do. Contrast that with the following situations.

> Michael's father was teaching him to brush his teeth. Michael was having difficulty getting the hang of it and kept questioning why he should brush his teeth. Each time his father brusquely admonished him, "Don't worry about why. Just do it."

> During the winter months, Melissa's parents insisted she take a children's vitamin every morning at breakfast. Sometimes she still had to be reminded to take the chewable tablet her mother put at her plate. When she questioned why she had to take the tablet, her mother would say, "Because it's good for you, sweetheart. Now take it."

Now, John may still not have much of an idea of what germs are, but at least he is starting to get that idea. Neither Michael nor Melissa is getting any input that indicates a line of reasoning. Melissa is being told her best interests are involved, but there's no information provided that supports the conclusion. There's nothing here that eventually contributes to her seeing where the benefit exists for her. And yet how easily she could have been provided some sense of that.

Get into the habit of taking your child's innate need for explanations into account. Why do you do the things you do? Why do you want your child to do things a certain way?

Understand the decisions you make as a parent. Look at their effect from your child's perspective. Then in explaining them, you'll have meaningful information the child can gradually learn to apply to later decision situations.

### HELPING YOUR CHILD TAKE INITIATIVES

A child's first conscious decisions will almost certainly relate to the routines that are built into everyday life. The choices to be made will primarily revolve around doing or not doing something your child is beginning to recognize as expected of him or her. Unlikely as yet to understand fully the consequences of an action on its own account, he or she probably will look only to those associated with limits you've set and reactions you've shown in the same or similar situations previously.

Given as he or she is to testing limits and, at this age, still prompted at least as much by impulse as by reason, a child will regularly overstep boundaries set on behavior. He or she will have to be brought back into line. How you react when this happens will greatly influence the attitude developing toward choices in general. What will you teach your child about consequences?

After building routines in a way that helps your child connect action and consequences, your next step is to help your child with his or her own initiatives. All children must be taught to realize that these, too, entail consequences.

Your child's capacity for initiatives will be limited at first. You may be surprised, nevertheless, at the range of initiatives possible for a child by the age of three.

As a parent, you can choose to either restrict or expand your child's sense of initiative. Since independence and responsibility are the eventual goals, your best option is to encourage initiative wherever your child shows a capacity for that. Again, you have to take a hand in that until abilities are sufficiently developed to allow you to trust the child more on his or her own.

Begin by isolating certain activities that your child can do with little or no direction from you. Identify routines already mastered to point the way.

Getting dressed provides a natural opportunity for your child to learn making choices of his or her own. At first you concentrate simply on establishing the routine (it's the same as with teaching a child to cross the street). First you have to go through the process with your child, in this case picking out articles of clothing and putting them on for him or her. Gradually you find your child is capable of putting things on with minimal assistance from you—pulling on socks, shirt, pants, etc. After a while, you will find you can lay out a set of clothes at night and simply leave it to your child to put them on in the morning. Now an element of routine depends on your child's initiative.

Of course, it will be important to allow for some failure. Preschool children do not always adhere to routine attentively. They may have some difficulty at times doing things they seemed to have mastered some time previous. Shirts may be put on backwards, and shoes will wind up on the wrong feet. But this is all part of the learning process.

Once your child has the hang of things in an area of routine and starts to take some initiative, list that as an accomplishment. Let him or her know you see it as such. Your child needs to feel a sense of achievement in order to be motivated toward further accomplishment.

Allowing your child more initiative in the area of achievement is a natural way of recognizing accomplishment. It also contributes to the further development of decision-related abilities. As a rule, young children are very quick to respond to this kind of recognition. They are eager to prove themselves able to handle things on their own.

Jerome was excited at the prospect of visiting his grandparents for a few days on his own. His parents had presented the visit as an opportunity for him to show the things he had learned to do for himself. The afternoon before his grandparents were to pick him up, his mother laid a small suitcase on his bed. If Jerome would pull out the things he wanted to take with him, she explained, she would later help him pack them into the suitcase. She reminded him to pick clothes he could play outdoors in and to include a couple favorite toys and games for indoors as well.

Here's a good example of prompting a child into taking an initiative that sharpens decision skills. Jerome gets to choose what to take along. He has a chance to follow his own priorities for a moment. He gets to make simple decisions that will influence the time he spends at his grandparents'.

Of course, it's very likely that Jerome doesn't yet have a complete sense of what he may need or will want to have with him. But that's not essential for allowing him the opportunity to take an initiative here. His mother will review his decisions; she can ensure that his oversights and omissions are corrected.

In a situation like this, *it's important that you not treat oversights or mistakes as failures.* See them rather as learning opportunities.

Suppose, for example, that Jerome's mother followed through by rejecting his choices, chiding him for his poor selection and then quickly packing articles she selected for him. In effect, she'd be telling him his choices were all unacceptable. She'd be emphasizing his lack of capability, and nothing in her actions would contribute to his developing a feeling of ability in this situation. She'd discourage rather than encourage Jerome when it comes to trying again.

Children are very sensitive to the humiliation of being judged incapable; it's not a feeling they like experiencing time and again.

When reviewing your child's decisions, look for positives. Compliment him or her on following through on an initiative. Reinforce good choices with explicit recognition. Use mistakes as opportunities to expand awareness of alternatives.

When Jerome's mother came in to see what he'd selected for his trip, she discovered he'd pulled out more than a dozen toys and games. His selection of clothing seemed haphazard. He'd picked out two favorite shirts and a hat he liked to wear outdoors, then added a pair of pants that should have gone into the laundry hamper.

His mother commented with a smile that she could see Jerome was looking forward to his visit, since he was taking some of his favorite things along. Then she pointed out that he'd need clean clothes for two days. She suggested to Jerome that they pretend he was getting dressed in the morning so they could see what he should have in his suitcase. After selecting the clothes—and putting aside the dirty trousers—she observed that he wouldn't have room for all the toys and games he'd picked out. She suggested he pick out just a few that he thought would be the most fun, and helped him narrow down his selection.

Note that in this situation the mother has referred back to a familiar routine to help Jerome get a better grip on what he's doing. And rather than pushing him aside to set things right, she's gone over the decisions involved with him. He retains some sense of initiative throughout, which provides a positive carryover. He isn't prompted into feelings of inadequacy that might inhibit him in subsequent situations like this.

Andrew, who was turning four, was asked what he would like to receive for his birthday. Over the course of the day, he mentioned ten different things he wanted, which his mother then recorded on a list. When his birthday came, he was disappointed to receive only two presents. His parents, angry at his attitude, threatened to take back the presents he'd been given if he didn't stop complaining.

Children have to be taught about priorities. They are very much creatures of the moment in the preschool years and tend to think in simple terms of wanting or not wanting. While they will demonstrate preferences early on, they commonly fail to recognize that preferences need to be identified in advance of a decision, since wants cannot all be accommodated at the same time.

Andrew's parents had the perfect opportunity for teaching something about priorities. After completing the list, they could easily have explained that it would be possible to give him only two of the items listed. Then they could have gone over the list item by item to help Andrew identify what he really wanted most. That would have provided a good lesson in how to recognize preferences and set priorities.

### RECOGNIZE YOUR CHILD'S LIMITATIONS

Although there is much you can do to start your preschool child on the road to making good decisions, the fact is that much of your preschooler's behavior will still be impulsive. Preschoolers grab for something they want the instant it occurs to them they want it. They will ignore a set routine because their minds are on something else at the moment.

Keep in mind that impulsive behavior is natural in young children. Don't expect your child to give up impulsive behavior just as soon as you've built routines, established limits, and begun to provide guidance in decisionmaking. It won't happen. It can't—your child lacks the necessary maturity for predictable self-control. He or she hasn't the sense of judgment that only experience provides, a point parents frequently forget in their expectations of young children.

Your child can only *begin* to respond to the guidance you're providing at this age. It will save you a lot of frustration if you keep your own expectations under control during this time.

Beware of pushing your child to achievement. That should not be your objective. Not only are you likely to suffer frustration; your child will, too. And he or she won't have the experience or insight that makes it possible to tolerate frustration easily. Unable to understand or meet expectations for the more mature behavior you are impatient to see adopted, your child will feel incapable. Rather than your guidance contributing to his or her approaching the world with expanding interest and confidence, it will prompt feelings of inadequacy. Your child may well adopt a pattern of avoiding new challenges to avoid having to deal with the frustrations they might expose him or her to.

> Sallie's parents were called into a conference at the day care center. Sallie had been involved in several fights with other children. Each time the day care coordinator had seen the fight, but not how it started. Since Sallie was involved each time, the coordinator had concluded that Sallie was somehow provoking the conflicts. After the conference, Sallie's parents told her that the family rule, which she knew about, was no fighting. They warned her that she would be severely punished if she got into another fight.

Any pattern of repeated misbehavior in young children is commonly a form of evidence that they haven't been able to break through some difficulty that faces them. The fact that guidelines have been established is not enough. The child may not find those sufficient to resolve conflicts or relieve frustrations that arise—they may only add to his or her feelings of dissatisfaction. In an effort to gain control of the situation on his or her own terms, the child resorts to whatever action seems likely at the moment to get what he or she wants or needs right then.

While it is appropriate to punish after a known family rule is violated, punishment by itself is a poor solution for a pattern of repeated misbehavior. In the case above, Sallie's parents should have explored why Sallie took the action she did. What prompted the impulse to strike out at classmates each time she experienced a certain threat or frustration?

The parents' task is to help Sallie find alternative ways other than fighting to deal with the situation. Invoking the consequences set for violating the established limit doesn't accomplish that by itself. Applied in isolation, it only tends to block the child from self-expression in the one way that's natural for the child, without providing an alternative route to expressing a need he or she evidently feels. Unless some alternative is identified, the result will be to bottle up feelings until emotional pressures build up to possibly explosive levels.

Use consequences to direct energies into constructive channels. Don't use them just to block misbehavior.

> Myron had quickly mastered simple tasks around the home that required a display of some initiative on his part. His father, deciding that Myron was exceptionally bright and would respond to additional developmental stimulus, set up a home reading program for him. Although demonstrating interest at first, Myron soon showed himself unenthusiastic for the daily routine of his father's program. His father, convinced that Myron was just being stubborn and only needed a firm hand to keep him at it, was stern and unremitting in his insistence that Myron continue in efforts to learn to read. Within a short time, the lesson period had developed into a time of uncomfortable confrontation between father and son.

The fact that a child shows a capacity for initiative in some areas does not mean he or she is automatically ready to take on something else. This particularly holds true for activities that require some use of intellect, as with reading, understanding numbers, or advance planning of some kind.

Trying to force development can backfire. Rather than turning your child on to a new interest, you may turn him or her off, thereby impeding later progress.

> Georgette's parents began introducing her to books when she was two years old. Every night before bedtime they read her a short children's story, and they also provided word and picture books they could read "with" her. Georgette soon began associating reading with special times of togetherness and regularly asked her parents to spend time reading with her.

There are ways to check out and develop your child's abilities in any area without pressuring him or her. Often it's simply a matter of exposing in an encouraging manner, then letting the child respond out of personal initiative to something that's presented as enjoyable.

Help—don't push—when it comes to prompting intellectual development. And don't worry if your child's interest or immediate accomplishments don't match that of some other child you know. Young children develop at different rates. Preschool is too soon to determine that your child has a learning disability or will prove a poor student (assuming your child is average with respect to general development).

Concentrate on opening up alternatives. Use consequences to direct attention to appropriate outlets for self-expression. Then build on your child's interests and enthusiasms. Recognize and acknowledge openly achievements made. Don't continually be emphasizing deficiencies and the need to remedy them.

And always take into account that at this age your child is still being introduced to the world. Your child won't always know what's expected of him or her even in situations that seem simple and clear-cut to you. Often he or she won't understand what's happening. At those times in particular, his or her reactions are likely to reflect an element of impulse. That's something to be alert to; it's not something to be alarmed about.

### WHEN OTHERS STEP IN—DAY CARE AND NURSERY SCHOOL

Families in which both parents pursue a career outside the home are increasingly common, even when there are preschool children. The past years have also seen a tremendous increase in the number of single parents who have to work to support themselves and dependent young children. This has resulted in great numbers of preschool children enrolled in day care centers and nursery schools. They spend long hours in an environment not totally under the parents' control. That time can either substantially contribute to or inhibit their developing a constructive sense of initiative when it comes to deciding on actions.

Parents who must or wish to enroll their child in a day care facility or nursery school should recognize that as a decision with consequences that bear directly upon the child.

## Day Care and Nursery School—What's the Difference?

Day care is pretty much what its name implies—an arrangement whereby someone assumes the responsibility of caring for the child during the hours the parent(s) is/are at work. It can be as simple as a babysitting service, but there are day care centers that will provide some program for learning.

State laws usually require anyone taking in children for a fee to be licensed. (There are, nevertheless, many instances of people with no license taking in children for day care.) The licensing laws do not generally require any specialized training on the part of those caring for the child. They aim primarily at ensuring that minimum standards are met in the facilities provided, that there's an acceptable ratio of adults to children, and that the day care providers have no police record.

Family day care centers customarily operate in a home environment, and this is often the easiest away-from-home experience for very young children to adjust to. However, these centers rarely offer a complete program of learning activities, and that can make them less suitable for a preschool child much past the age of three who would benefit from a more stimulating environment.

Most nursery schools are licensed by the state as educational facilities, with those in charge of the children required to meet certain professional qualifications. They provide a basic learning program, although what that is varies considerably from school to school.

Set up as they are on a more formal basis, nursery schools generally enroll greater numbers of children than family-type day care centers. The environment can prove stimulating to the more mature preschool child, but it may be unsettling for the younger, less self-assured child.

### When Can I Enroll My Child?

Parents with children younger than age two and a half are usually going to be looking for day care for their child. That is often available in some form even for children who are still infants. (Your options, of course, depend upon where you live and what is actually available in your area.) Many nursery schools will not enroll children before age two and a half, although specific minimum age requirements vary.

If your circumstances do not require you to enroll your child in a day care facility or nursery school, you will have leeway in coming to a decision here. In particular, you will be able to take into account whether or not your child is really prepared to spend time away from home in the care of others. Your decision will probably revolve around whether or not to send your preschooler to nursery school, as you will most likely be handling day care needs until you think your child is mature enough to start in a program that offers more structured learning opportunities.

Here are questions to ask yourself when evaluating your child's readiness for nursery school.

- Is your child able to understand and follow simple directions?
- Is he or she attentive to family routines?
- Does your child recognize limits and generally understand the consequences of violating limits?
- Is he or she able to exercise some initiative in completing tasks or making elementary choices?
- Is your child curious about the world away from home (as opposed to fearful and frightened of unfamiliar people and places)?

Deciding whether your child is ready is less a matter of age than of whether you feel you can satisfactorily answer these and similar questions. If you can't wholeheartedly answer these questions *yes*, your child may have difficulty making an adjustment to nursery school. Consider postponing his or her enrollment until a readiness for the experience is more apparent.

### How Do I Choose Where to Enroll My Child?

Whether it's a day care facility or a nursery school of any kind, *always* assure yourself that minimum sanitary and safety standards are met. *Always* confirm that there is adequate supervision and that whoever will be in charge of your child is properly qualified. Your best approach is to make sure the facility is registered with or licensed by the state, as licensing requirements include attention to sanitation, to safety, and to minimum credentials for personnel supervising children. That includes specifying a requisite ratio of adult staff to the number of children enrolled.

Naturally, you also have to take your own situation into account. There's the question of costs and what you can afford. Do you need or want your child to attend for a full day five days a week, or will part-time enrollment be sufficient? Are you looking for a particular focus when it comes to value or orientation—e.g., religious affiliation or a particular emphasis on development of your child's learning abilities?

Of course the question of what's available in your area will also influence your decision.

Treat the selection of where to enroll your child as the important decision it is. Identify the *values* important to you in connection with your child's well-being and development. Identify the *goal* you have with respect to what enrollment is to accomplish. Take time to discover the *alternatives* available, and gather and collate what *information* you can about each. What *consequences* in terms of effect on your child do you see attached to the choices possible? Once you've identified desirables and weighed the risks in any choice, make your decision, aiming at the best balance between benefits anticipated and risks you are prepared to accept. Take *action*—enroll your child. Then *review* the outcome. Be ready to make adjustments whenever it becomes evident that your child's best interests call for those.

A major objective in your choice will be to ensure your child's decisionmaking abilities are stimulated. What should you take into consideration when evaluating alternatives in this context?

*The staff.* Those in charge of or assisting in handling the children should:

- Be attentive to the children at all times.
- Demonstrate a caring involvement with them.
- Take time to explain routines and expectations.
- Listen to children's expressions of feelings and needs.
- Encourage and help them take initiatives and make choices.
- Clearly set limits on behavior that is unacceptable and establish appropriate consequences to constructively redirect behavior.
- Show flexibility in their response to situations that require adult intervention.

*The program.* The activities offered should promote your child's developing increased proficiency in taking constructive initiatives when it comes to deciding on actions. They should:

- Hold the child's interest without that being forced.
- Be easy enough to allow the child a sense of achievement without requiring constant adult intervention.
- Be challenging enough to encourage further development of the child's abilities.
- Be diverse enough to provide continuing stimulation and opportunities for new initiative.
- Encourage development of social skills—playing together, undertaking simple projects in cooperation with others.

- Reinforce basic social values—sharing, respect for property, consideration for others.
- Reflect a recognition that each child is an individual with his or her own unique needs and talents.

## Observe for Yourself

Once you've identified "core" alternatives (ruled out possibilities that clearly do not meet your standards or fit your needs), your best bet is to arrange to visit those nursery schools. Work it out so that you have the opportunity to discuss your concerns with staff members. Inquire about staff qualifications. What values do they seek to emphasize? What are their goals for the children enrolled? What routines do they set up for the children?

Also ask to spend an hour or so quietly observing staff and children in interaction. Be as unobtrusive as possible—you want as much of a "fly on the wall" view of things as possible.

Leave your child at home on these visits. Otherwise you will be too absorbed in your child and his or her reactions to assess what's happening in this new environment you are evaluating.

Pay close attention to the children in particular.

- In general, do they seem happily occupied and involved in what's going on?
- How do they react to staff members? With eager friendliness or hesitant timidity?
- Do they seem to have a clear sense of routines?
- How do they get along with one another?
- Do they appear to follow rules that have been established?
- Do they have obvious responsibilities in areas like cleaning up or preparing for activities?

Once you've identified a likely nursery school in which to enroll your child, ask to bring your child for a visit. This provides a nonthreatening introduction to a completely new experience. Your child will see your interest; that will be reassuring. Your presence enables your child to observe what's going on and develop an interest in that without being preoccupied with fears of being left alone in a strange place.

### Your Child's First Days

You want your child to look forward to nursery school, not to go kicking and screaming in protest. How you present the idea of enrollment to him or her can make a big difference here.

Take a positive approach. Explain to your child that he or she is big enough to go to school. Present it as a form of recognition for past achievements. Let your child hear you talk it up to others in that light.

Don't warn of adjustments that may be necessary. Don't fret aloud about difficulties that may occur. Don't show a worried concern that your child might not be able to adjust to this different environment. If you display those kind of nervous fears about what will happen, imagine what your child will conclude.

It's still possible your child will be uncomfortable during the first days of school. Reassure your child that you care. Express confidence in his or her ability to make the adjustment. Ask your child to bring home something made at school as a sign of what he or she can do.

Don't take the approach demonstrated in this example:

> Rita came home from her first few days at nursery school whiny and fretful. She dogged her mother's tracks, all the while asking for attention of one sort or other. She cried in the morning when her mother took her to school, clinging to her mother's arm and loudly wailing in protest at being left. Her mother, embarrassed by the unwanted attention Rita's behavior attracted, scolded her sharply, telling her not to be such a baby, then drove away hurriedly once Rita's teacher had her in hand.

Rita's mother is only adding to her child's adjustment difficulties. By her actions she's almost certainly confirming Rita's obvious fears about being abandoned somehow. In Rita's eyes, school probably seems a place of exile from the security she was accustomed to at home previously. Rather than her attendance being presented as a sign of achievement, she experiences it as some sort of punishment. She may very well regress to more infantile behavior in an effort to regain her previous security.

### Recognizing Problems

Despite taking every care and precaution, it is still possible that problems may arise that require your intervention. The signs will be fairly obvious once you know what to look for.

Your child will provide the best indication of how things are going. After a first week or two of adjustment, your child should begin to show a greater sense of ease with the idea of going to school. After a month or two, you should be getting positive feedback. Your child should:

- Demonstrate a ready willingness to go off to school in the morning.
- Give spontaneous positive reports of experiences in school. (You do have to allow for occasional unhappiness.)
- Show an increasing ability to get along with other children.
- Demonstrate an increased sense of initiative along constructive lines.
- Show a greater awareness of and more lively interest in the world in general.

*Something is wrong if:*

- Your child consistently expresses unhappiness or anxiety about going to school.
- You get frequent reports of your child's misbehaving in school.

- You get frequent reports of your child's being unable to adjust.
- Your child fails to progress in showing initiative—and seems to regress in a particularly uncharacteristic fashion.
- Your child increasingly shrinks from contact with new people or new situations.

When you see these signs, you will know some adjustment is called for. However, keep in mind that it is sometimes a problem in the home as much as a problem at school that is contributing to your child's difficulty. Look at what's happening at home as well as into what's happening at school to be sure you aren't part of the problem.

Talk to your child. Listen to what he or she has to say. Your child may not be able to express himself or herself well, but you will usually be able to pick up some clue to what the trouble is. In conversation, avoid feeding your child loaded questions. "Is your teacher mean to you?" can win a "yes" nod if the child thinks that's the answer you're looking for. "How do you like your teacher?" "Why do you feel that way?" are nonleading questions that will get you the child's answer more surely.

Speak to your child's teacher. What does the teacher think may be the problem? Does the teacher in fact see a problem? What does he or she feel will help your child make a better adjustment?

If this can be arranged, visit the school again. Can you observe what is happening with your child without your presence proving too intrusive? Perhaps it might be a good idea to visit the class one day without your child in attendance. Reexamine the interaction between staff and children. Look at how the children relate to each other. Does it seem a staff member or an aggressive child could be creating a difficulty? Look for tie-ins with what your child has told you.

Bobby showed an increasing reluctance to go to school. At the same time, his teacher reported that Bobby was proving "uncooperative" and "disrespectful" when at school. His parents were surprised, as they'd never experienced any major problem with Bobby's behavior at home. When observing the class situation before enrolling him, they'd particularly noted how well behaved children in the class were. Bobby had evidently formed a dislike for his teacher. In speaking with his teacher, it became evident that her expectations of Bobby in learning activities led her to push him to achievements he was not yet capable of.

When there's a problem at school, it's not necessarily a case of the school or the teacher deliberately mistreating children or taking an indifferent approach to children's needs. (If either evidently does, then you are well advised to turn immediately to an alternative arrangement.) Speak with the teacher about possible adjustments that will help your child have a more positive experience. Since the interests of the child are paramount, the teacher should prove flexible in his or her consideration of those. If the teacher is not, it may be advisable to consider other arrangements.

> Kevin couldn't seem to adjust to nursery school. He went under protest every morning. His teacher reported frustration at finding no way to get him to participate with interest in class activities. Was there a situation in the home that might have introduced some element of change that was providing Kevin difficulty? His parents could think of only one possibility: There was a new baby in the family. In fact they had in part decided on nursery school for Kevin in order to allow his mother to concentrate her attention on the baby without at the same time having to attend to Kevin, too.

Being sent to school at the arrival of a new baby can make a child feel he or she is being replaced. Unless the parents find a positive way to "reincorporate" the child into the family unit, this can result in adjustment difficulties and possible misbehavior aimed at asserting a now-outdated sense of place in the family. Other family situations that may have an adverse effect on the child's overall behavior inside and outside the home include marital tensions, serious illness in the family, or the death of a family member.

In responding to difficulties your preschool child is having, don't concentrate solely on providing solutions for the child. Involve your child in the process of deciding on and making adjustments. Help him or her to understand changes in the family situation or in the world in general. Encourage your child to adapt to changes in routine. Provide guidance in taking new initiatives.

When it comes to the increased role others play in your child's life, ascertain their attitude and approach to his or her needs. You want their efforts to complement yours when it comes to educating for responsible independence.

The preschool years may not seem the most significant when it comes to teaching your child about decisions. Don't be misled. A good start in these years will give your child a valuable head start in establishing a self-confident capability to cope with and relate to the world throughout his or her life. A bad start can introduce habits of behavior and unrealistic expectations that inhibit the development of good judgment and that ultimately impose consequences upon the child that work to his or her disadvantage. What you do has critical impact. So does your child's first experience of extended time spent outside the home.

# 13

## The Grade School Years

By the age of five or six most children can express themselves fairly well when it comes to basic needs and wants. They are able to follow a wide range of simple directions. They have developed sufficient physical coordination to handle objects with some dexterity. Most children have incorporated a diversity of routines into their own standard repertory of behaviors, among them feeding, dressing, and attending to toilet functions without need of adult intervention. Many have begun to exercise some judgment of their own, doing or not doing things with some awareness of consequences that may be involved.

Now most children are ready for school. Suddenly their world expands beyond the boundaries of the home. Parents retain primary responsibility for their child's well-being, but for long hours every week others exercise a legal authority *in loco parentis*—in the place of the parent.

### THE ADJUSTMENT TO SCHOOL

The shift to the new environment of school is probably the biggest adjustment any child has to make in the preteen years. Your child goes from the familiar setting of the home to a

183

setting that is unfamiliar, where he or she is one small individual in the midst of a seeming host of strangers.

Children who have nursery school experience generally make a fairly easy adjustment to grade school. They've been introduced to the reality of adults other than their parents giving them direction. They've already begun to develop the social skills for getting along with peers. They'll find at least some familiar routines, and the school situation itself will not seem so strange.

A child who has not been to nursery school has none of this preparation for the school years ahead. His or her life has been entirely centered on the home.

If this is your child's first experience "away from home," there's a lot you can do to make adjustments easier. Basically, your approach should be the same as that recommended for parents enrolling their preschool children in nursery school (see pages 175–182). Present beginning school positively, as a sign of maturity achieved. Avoid dire warnings of difficulties ahead. Don't overemphasize the adjustments to be made— your child may look upon going to school with foreboding. Your aim is building confidence. You want your child to look forward to the challenge of this new adventure, not to dread it as some ordeal that lies ahead.

On the other hand, don't get too carried away. Some parents work so hard at expressing enthusiasm and developing motivation in their child that they overdo it. A child can easily feel overwhelmed by the expectations implicit in his or her parents' cheerleading exuberance. Your child will feel pressured to perform at a time when his or her energies are necessarily focused simply on adjusting. If the adjustment proves at all difficult, your child may experience a sense of failure, of having let his or her parents down. And that is likely only to complicate the adjustment a child has to make.

Be positive. Be reassuringly matter-of-fact. Don't plant an apprehension in your child's mind that he or she won't be able to cope with the new demands of a new situation. But don't set it up so that your child feels guilty about a difficulty he or she is having, because somehow you've given the impression you expect perfection from Day One.

Jean's parents went to great lengths to ensure she looked forward to her first day at school. They told her all the wonderful things she'd be doing. They bought her a complete new wardrobe and equipped her with a shiny pencil box. So they were surprised to hear her say after less than a week of school that she didn't want to go anymore. Sending her off to school became an occasion for tearful scenes of reluctance. Her parents steadfastly projected an optimistic image of all that school had to offer her, but nothing they could think to say aroused any corresponding enthusiasm in her.

Jean's parents are trying too hard to be positive. In effect, they're refusing to acknowledge that Jean is having a real difficulty. Their optimism neither comforts nor reassures. How can it? It runs counter to Jean's experience. She's having trouble adjusting to a situation that is uncomfortable for her, and they keep telling her how wonderful it is and how much she should be enjoying it. Something's off, and Jean may well feel her parents are really telling her she's off.

It's no contribution to your child's ability to cope to be told there's no cause for difficulty. That you don't understand the problem he or she is having and see no reason for it doesn't lessen its impact on your child.

Overcoming a problem requires dealing with it somehow. You can't make it go away by pretending it's not there.

Martin's parents were surprised at the difficulty he was having adjusting to school. Their other children, all older than Martin, had adjusted easily. But every day Martin went to school unwillingly, and his teacher reported he cried long periods every day despite all efforts to draw him into the activities of the class. When they spoke with Martin about his school behavior, he only became sullen and withdrawn.

Children do not always know what makes adjusting to school difficult for them. Parents, relying on feedback from the child for some cue as to where reassurance is needed, feel stymied. How do you help when you can't tell why your child is behaving as he or she is?

Naturally, the more you know about why your child feels uncomfortable and insecure, the easier it is to decide what to do about it. So listening to your child's complaints and remarks is important. However, there's something you can do to help even if what upsets him or her isn't exactly clear.

> Martin's parents decided on an approach of establishing positive consequences to encourage more effort on his part to adjust to school. They told him that if he made it through three days without complaint or crying, he would earn an hour of "special activity" time with his father on Saturday afternoon. If he made it through a whole week, he could choose a special activity for the entire afternoon—a trip to the zoo, a drive to his grandparents', etc. They asked Martin's teacher to provide him a note of achievement whenever either period had passed without difficulty.

A child may have difficulty making the transition to school for a variety of reasons. Some relate to fear of the strangeness of the situation, some to a fear of being abandoned. Some grow out of the failure to see that school offers satisfactions comparable to those your child was used to at home.

A positive approach like that taken by Martin's parents helps in each case. With the prospect of a desired activity before him, Martin will tend to focus less strongly on his fears. He'll at least have a motivation for standing up to them as best he can. Looking forward to a special promised time together will allay anxiety that somehow he is being cast aside. And having an incentive he understands for adjustment efforts will prompt a more open attitude toward school itself. If nothing else, he can now look at it as a challenge to take on rather than as something not to be endured without protest.

This kind of approach provides a valuable lesson. As we've previously noted, young children commonly look for instant gratification when making behavior decisions. Children who learn early on that bearing up under discomfort can lead to tangible benefit later on will be more thoughtful sooner in making choices between instant gratification and the prospect of a benefit to be enjoyed later.

### FREEDOM AND IDENTITY

Although entering school will require your child to make considerable and rapid adjustments, it will also provide a kind of freedom he or she has not had before.

For many youngsters, school provides the first go-it-alone experience in exercising skills learned at home. There's no longer a caring parent looking over the child's shoulder, ready to head off any problems that might present themselves. As one child in a group that may number as many as thirty, your child won't get the individual attention a parent can provide at home. How things go from here depends increasingly on your child's willingness and ability to take initiatives, to follow through on his or her own once instruction has been given.

Look at what faces a child entering school. He or she has to

- Accept new authority figures
- Learn new routines
- Follow new rules
- Face new consequences
- Apply instruction to unfamiliar tasks
- Learn to make friends
- Deal with peer pressures

All these situations provide a range of choice possibilities that your child has not previously faced. Adjusting to those is task enough for any child, but the shift into a totally new environment for long hours of the day adds a complication. Your child not only has to face new challenges in the area of behavior but at the same time must find his or her place in a new, vastly expanded world.

As long as a child's world is centered on the home, he or she isn't apt to be particularly troubled by conflicts about identity.

Position in the family will be clearly defined, and your child will have developed habits that correspond to his or her sense of place as a family member. Your child knows what's expected of him or her and what can be expected of others.

The new world of school requires adjusting to a different role as well as to a different setting. And that can create something of an identity crisis. Confused about new expectations from teachers and peers, your child may well develop uncharacteristic behavior in an effort to make a place for himself or herself in school.

> Martha, an early achiever at home, surprised her parents by coming home with reports of poor performance in her schoolwork throughout her first year of school. Her teacher reported that Martha did not follow instructions well and that she tended to stay on the fringe of group activities rather than participate fully. When her parents spoke with her about her disappointing performance, Martha complained of not liking school. Her parents told her she had no choice about liking school and warned her that continued poor performance would result in loss of privileges she enjoyed.

Martha's parents are making an all too common mistake. They're assuming that telling a child that he or she has no choice will prompt him or her into greater effort, particularly if that message is reinforced with a threat. They're counting on a fear of negative consequences to motivate a child to positive achievement.

This kind of approach does often lead to results more in line with parents' expectations. However, it doesn't help the child gain a more positive perspective on the school experience. Without this positive perspective the child may work only toward a minimum level of achievement, not toward developing his or her full potential.

Martha does have a choice, regardless of what her parents tell her. She may not be free to skip school, but much of the initiative she takes in school is up to her. Her parents would stimulate her to greater achievement much more surely if they made the effort to help her find her place in the classroom.

Once she identifies herself routinely as a student and accepts that identity, she will take more initiatives that lead to achievement, in contrast to previous actions pointing up her feelings of alienation in school.

It's unfortunate how many children come to see themselves as prisoners of the school system rather than as trainees for an adult life that satisfies their own aspirations. The prisoner perspective invariably inclines them to resist following routines that build intellectual skills they can use to advantage in later years.

You can do a lot to help your child recognize that education provides meaningful opportunities by employing a variation on the Real You Collage introduced in Chapter 8 (see page 87). Focus on benefits and the chance for gain. Help erase the prisoner mentality by showing how constructive initiative gets your child more of what he or she wants even now. Point to the freedom to achieve to offset feelings that school is an environment entirely characterized by restrictions.

When you can give your child the needed uninterrupted attention, sit down together and get him or her to respond to these questions:

- What do I like to do?
- Whom do I like being with?
- What makes me feel good?
- What makes me feel sad?
- What makes me mad?
- What do I want to be when I grow up?

Let your child answer in his or her own words; resist feeding your child the responses you want to hear. Write down the answers in a space under each question. If you think some detail is being overlooked, try to elicit that without forcing it. (Look back to page 87 for help here.)

Once you're satisfied your child has given as complete an answer as he or she can to each question, introduce for consideration the question: "How can school help?"

Surprising as it may seem, it's not unusual for young children in the early school years to fail to see any connection between school and what they hope to experience or would like to do. This exercise, taking an explicitly positive approach, can help them make that connection. Every positive connection you make builds a more positive outlook toward school itself.

Here's an example of some responses and connections a six-year-old might make in this activity:

| *What do I like to do?* | *How school can help* |
| --- | --- |
| 1. Play with my train set | 1. Help me find out more about railroads and how real trains are run. |
| 2. Go to the zoo | 2. Teach me about different kinds of animals and where and how they live. |
| 3. Help Dad in his workshop | 3. Teach me about measures for making sure things come out the right size. |
| 4. Watch cartoons on TV | 4. Learn to draw; discover how cartoons are made. |
| 5. Visit Grandma and Grandpa | 5. Teach me to write, so I can write letters to them. |

You won't necessarily be able to make a connection between every response and what school can provide to broaden the experience, but you should be able to make enough connections to show an immediate positive potential in schoolwork. Once your child sees that school does tie into things and activities that have meaning, he or she is more likely to develop further connections without your help.

But don't leave it at an intellectual exercise. Prompt your child into taking new initiatives with an immediate follow-up that reinforces a more positive view of what school can do for him or her. However, don't take an authoritarian approach, or the whole exercise can backfire. Your child may well come to see himself or herself more than ever forced into activities others prescribe, which negates any sense of initiative that might otherwise develop.

Carl's report card indicated he was not performing up to expectations in his schoolwork. When his parents called his teacher for details, she told them he habitually doodled and dreamed rather than kept up with his lessons. Carl's response to questions about his schoolwork was that he hated school. His parents asked him to tell them what he would rather do. What did he think he might like to be when he grew up? Carl mentioned his love for animals and his ambition to be an animal doctor someday. Taking their cue from that, they took Carl to the public library and helped him pick out a children's book on elephants, the animal that fascinated him most. Throughout the next week they set aside twenty minutes each day to coach him in reading the book after a brief review of standard school assignments aimed at building his reading vocabulary.

Carl's parents are taking an approach that help him relate schoolwork to personal interests and ambitions. They're not simply pointing out possibilities to him. They're getting involved, working with him to develop a more positive orientation toward school assignments. In essence, they're providing a guiding hand to help him establish a new routine, recognizing that a grade school child sometimes needs much the same help in that area as a preschool child needs.

### THE PARENT AND THE "OUTSIDE" WORLD

It's all too common for parents to leave their children's education up to the schools. The tendency is to assume that teachers will make sure children learn what they are supposed to.

That assumption only reinforces any tendency a child may have to see school as an environment apart from the real world. It also overlooks the realities of the classroom. Teachers can set standards and push for performance that measures up to those. They cannot ensure every child is working up to the level of his or her abilities—each child retains initiative there. Teachers have to spread their attention across a group of youngsters, which means that individual needs can go unnoticed and/or unattended. And that's not to mention what happens when a teacher proves more or less indifferent to anything besides a minimal daily routine that gets him or her through the week with the least effort and trouble.

The behavior your child adopts in school has a considerable choice element to it. Attitudes toward schoolwork can be either positive or negative, depending on how your child interprets the classroom experience. Performance can reflect minimal effort or a determination to excel. Relations with peers can show if your child is more concerned to conform with their expectations than to follow behavioral guidelines established in the family setting.

It can be dangerous simply to assume your child will automatically apply standards set in the home to behavior outside the home. Other settings, with their different routines and a different cast of characters, often make it appear appropriate to adopt different standards of behavior. Parents who don't take an active interest in what happens at school encourage the view that school is a world unto itself where different rules apply. That can lead to later shocked discovery that their child, a "good boy" or "good girl" at home, assumes a different personality outside the home. In deciding on behavior, your child may be acting on impulse or taking a "me first" approach to things that wouldn't be acceptable at home.

> Jesse's parents were dismayed when his fourth-grade teacher reported she'd caught him cheating on tests and discovered he was bribing another student to do his math homework for him. Confronted with this knowledge, Jesse protested that everyone shared answers and that his other teachers hadn't cared how homework was done, as long as it was turned in. His parents pointed out to him that cheating in this way was a form of lying and that he knew the family rule against lying. Furthermore, his inappropriate use of allowance money to bribe other students showed he was not yet mature enough to handle money without parental supervision. Until he gave evidence of greater maturity, his allowance would be restricted, with money given him only for specified uses his parents could monitor.

Jesse's parents have an obvious sense of how to link actions and consequences. It's clear they expect standards of behavior established in the home to provide guidelines for behavior outside the home. However, if Jesse's been following a divergent standard at school for any length of time, they've probably not been sufficiently attentive to what's been happening with him in school. They've relied too heavily on teachers who haven't been concerned or able to uphold a standard considered fundamental in the home.

These first years of sustained contact with the outside world are crucial ones. Your child will be out of your sight for extended periods of time, not just at school, but playing outdoors with friends or just roaming around to see what's happening in the neighborhood. Lots of opportunities arise during these periods for behavior choices that no adult will supervise. It's impossible for you always to know what your child is up to, but you can too readily abdicate any responsibility for his or her behavior. While you can't know from moment to moment what your child may be involved in, you should have a reasonably accurate sense of what kind of things he or she is likely to be doing. All it takes is developing a habit of communication that provides you a reasonably accurate sense of

- What your child does in school
- Who your child's friends are
- What your child's usual activities are
- Where your child is when he or she is not at home or at school
- Whether or not your child is having difficulty in school or with peers
- How your child handles him- or herself in general outside the home

Should you discover your child is having difficulty or behaving unacceptably outside the home, follow the same procedures you'd use for getting things back on track inside the home.

Wendell's parents learned that he had damaged public property along with a group of boys he hung out with in a nearby park. They imposed consequences they felt fit the action, putting him on a strict curfew after school until such time as he showed himself ready to behave more responsibly. A few days later they learned that none of the other boys were being punished, and Wendell protested that his punishment was therefore unfair. Confused and unwilling to take a stand that the other parents' inaction made seem overly harsh, Wendell's parents decided to drop the consequences they'd imposed.

It is very easy for parents to yield to the pressures of what other parents are doing (or, in this case, not doing). But yielding to this kind of pressure can be very counterproductive when it comes to teaching responsible behavior.

Refer back to your family philosophy when it comes to your reactions to behavior outside the home. Make it clear to your child that the family philosophy spells out standards of behavior family members are expected to follow outside the home as well as within the home, at least to the extent possible. What other people do in a situation like the above is their decision. Your concern is to do what makes sense to you and your family, and your child has clear guidelines in the family philosophy to know what limits to observe in behavior outside the home and what consequences to expect when those limits are exceeded.

When the consequences established for unacceptable behavior reinforce the lesson you are trying to teach, stick with them. Your child's future behavior is at stake. If you get an argument about others' lack of concern in an area you are concerned about, simply point out that you feel this lack of concern is not appropriate and why you feel that way. Your child will realize his or her friends' parents have the responsibility for guiding them into appropriate behavior; he or she can't expect you to do so. And if you are careful to express positive expectations and don't just leave it at imposing negative consequences, your child will sense that your disciplinary action reflects a caring concern for what happens within your own family.

## KEEPING COMMUNICATIONS LINES OPEN

One reason for keeping communications lines between you and your child open is to be sure your child doesn't develop behavior patterns outside the home that he or she knows are unacceptable in your home. But there's something more to take into account. Your child needs to know that you care about everything that happens, even when you are not around, because you care about him or her. Then, too, your child may from time to time experience a problem he or she can't easily define or resolve but is reluctant to admit to you.

Eight-year-old Denise had trouble making friends. Her parents had never heard her complain of this, so were surprised when one day she tearfully blurted out, "Nobody likes me!" They had observed that she was shy with other children but never thought to discuss her relations with other children with her. They'd assumed she was going through a phase she'd soon grow out of.

Have Denise's parents used the various opportunities available to keep in touch with her relationships outside of their home? Everyday family routines provide natural opportunities to discuss what's happening in your child's world. We've identified a number of these previously—mealtimes together, shared family activities, time either parent spends alone with a child, etc. An inventory of family routines will point to the opportunities you have to keep up with what's happening with your child. (See the Family-Routine Review on pages 84–85.) Then it's a matter of following the guidelines set out in Chapter 10 for ensuring your efforts at communication are effective.

Keep in mind, however, that your child is not always a wholly reliable source of information. Like Denise, your child may not want to admit a problem to you. Or like Jesse, in the exam-

ple on page 192, your child may be following a double standard without wanting to bring that to your attention. If you
make the effort to maintain regular, open communication with
your child, you will probably note what subjects elicit little or
no reaction and/or inconsistencies in remarks that are made.
Those observations may clue you in to problems and problem
behavior that require parental intervention—either supportive or disciplinary action on your part.

Even so, you will be in an isolation circle (see page 100) if
you rely only on the information your child provides you, and
that will be true no matter how open the lines of communication are. You need other perspectives to provide you information necessary for ensuring you respond promptly and appropriately to situations that call for parental intervention.

### Maintaining School Contacts

Most grade schools make an effort to keep parents in touch
with the educational program set up for their child and to alert
them to problems their child may be having in school. Schools
will schedule special times for parent-teacher conferences; set
up "back to school" nights; sponsor extracurricular activities/
events that parent and child can attend or participate in together; and encourage parent involvement in the local Parent-
Teacher's Association (PTA).

In addition, most schools encourage parents to contact
teachers and/or administration for consultations about progress their child is making or difficulties he or she may be having, whether those are academic or center on behavior.

You will find it much easier to follow your child's progress
in school if you keep a line of contact of your own there, rather than simply rely on your child's report of what's happening.
It's not a matter of calling in for a report every day. All you
really need do is establish contact with the teacher and the
school through the opportunities provided, so that you know
what the educational program is and whom to refer to when

you have questions about your child's academic performance or behavior.

## A Peer Parenting Group

As your child increasingly develops personal lines of contact outside the family, you'll find your child beginning to observe and react to the differences he or she sees between the routines of your home and others. Sometimes those differences will be very real; other times they will be more apparent than real. In either case, your child will increasingly refer to what he or she sees happening in other homes when questioning the routines and limits established in your home.

Renee's parents insisted she spend at least an hour each evening with her schoolwork. They felt this was a necessary minimum for ensuring she kept up with her lessons. Renee often announced she'd completed her assignments well before the hour was up and repeatedly protested having to stay with her schoolwork through the time allotted. No one else in her class had to follow this rule, and she maintained it was unfair for her parents to enforce a different routine than her friends' parents did.

Renee's parents had joined a peer parenting group and brought up their difficulty with her in one of the group meetings. They found several other parents in agreement that the routine established was a good one. Somebody suggested allowing Renee free reading time to finish out her hour time period whenever she'd completed her assigned work. That would provide educational benefit while moderating frustration at having to sit over work she'd already completed.

It's often difficult for parents to know how to respond to reports suggesting they're out of step with what's happening in other families. And sometimes it's difficult to know just what is happening in other families.

Joining together in a peer parenting group—that is, coming together on a regular basis with other parents whose children are roughly the same age or in the same school—provides a means of breaking out of the isolation circle as a parent. You establish a line of contact that tells you how others respond to situations you face as a parent. You have a network of support when faced with decisions on limits to establish or enforce.

To put it in decision-related terms, a peer parenting group provides you a forum in which to:

- Reexamine values and goals you've established in your family.
- Develop new alternatives for responding to situations that call for action on your part.
- Gain new information about situations that affect you in relations with your child or that have a bearing on your child's relationships outside the home.
- Reevaluate consequences you've established in connection with limits on behavior.
- Establish new guidelines for taking action; reconfirm guidelines that either you or your child now question.
- Review decisions you've made as a parent.

Check with your school's counseling office to find out if there is a peer parenting group already established in your locale. (It may be termed a parents' discussion group, parent support group, or go by some similar name—the counselor will be able to tell you.) If so, find out where and when it meets and how it functions. See about attending a meeting as an observer, if you want to check it out before committing yourself to join.

If there's no group established in your community or you don't feel that what's available is satisfactory, think about starting one of your own. You may want to begin with a small group of parents you already know who have children about your child's age. If you are active in church or a community group, you may want to operate within the framework of that organization.

You don't have to go formal; an informal discussion among a few parents can be as helpful as any preset program. However, to obtain full benefit from your group, you should adhere to a few basic guidelines.

*1. Set up some kind of regular schedule for getting together.* Parents should know when and where meetings will be held. Setting a schedule of dates that group members agree to in advance also strengthens the commitment to participate regularly. (Rotating meetings among the homes of participating group members can be effective if no central meeting location is readily available.)

*2. Keep the meeting focused on parenting concerns.* The easiest way to do this is to set up a minimal agenda. This provides two benefits. It guards against the meeting turning into nothing more than a neighborhood kaffeeklatsch. It minimizes awkward silences in which everyone waits for someone else to open the discussion. (Many peer parenting groups have found that enlisting a professional in the area of child care or family relations to serve as moderator helps keep focus where it should be.)

*3. Outline a basic process/line of approach that all parents agree on for dealing with problems they face.* Agreeing on a common approach ensures that everyone in the group is speaking the same "language" when discussing situations facing them. Parents will find themselves working through situations with common objectives in sight. (I find the decisionmaking framework particularly suitable, as it provides an easy-to-follow line of approach all can agree on and yet allows for individual differences from parent to parent. It also works well in conjunction with a focus on any life philosophy that a parent group may want to affirm, for example emphasizing Jewish or Christian values and traditions.)

*4. Make some provision for out-of-group contact between parents.* Parenting is a day-to-day responsibility, not something that dovetails neatly into a schedule of periodic review. A parent may need information on a situation that unexpectedly arises; he or she may want some help developing alternatives for action that cannot be postponed until after a next meeting.

Everyone should feel that support from group members is available on a day-to-day basis. (That's not to say contact should be limited to circumstances of need. Social contacts are often helpful, too.)

If you as a parent are regularly in contact with other parents of children your child's age, you'll undoubtedly find that informal contacts can provide many if not all of the benefits of a peer parenting group. That's alright, too. Look back at the benefits listed on page 198 for peer parenting groups. If you find your informal contacts provide you all of these, then you may not need the support a peer parenting group can provide.

However, many parents—especially in households where both hold outside jobs—are not routinely in contact with other adults as parents. In that case, there's a much greater likelihood that they will unwittingly find themselves isolated as far as what is happening with their child outside the home. Joining a peer parenting group then becomes a valuable means of establishing contacts supportive of their efforts to raise a responsible child.

### BUILDING YOUR CHILD'S DECISION AWARENESS

In everything you do, a long-range focus on parenting toward independence entails guiding your child into increasing reliance on the decision framework. You want your child to:

- Learn what a decision is, why it is important, and who should make it.
- Discover what is really important to him or her personally.
- Think about the impact his or her actions can have on others.
- Become sensitive in general to the world beyond home and parents.
- Reckon with the fact of consequences attached to every action taken.

It may help you to take a quick audit of your child's present decision-related skills and attitudes.

| Skill Area | What Exists Now | What Could Be Improved |
|---|---|---|
| Has an accurate sense of strengths and weaknesses | _____ | _____ |
| Has the ability to think ahead | _____ | _____ |
| Knows the rules of the world beyond the home and parents | _____ | _____ |
| Shows sensitivity to people and things affecting and affected by his or her behavior choices | _____ | _____ |
| Distinguishes between immediate wants and long-term goals | _____ | _____ |
| Distinguishes between what others expect and what he or she wants and stands up for his or her own opinions | _____ | _____ |
| Understands what it means to live with consequences | _____ | _____ |
| Plans ahead and accepts accountability for a failure to plan ahead | _____ | _____ |
| Knows why certain things yield good and bad feelings | _____ | _____ |
| Knows what is important to family, to peers, and to self | _____ | _____ |
| Works out ways to resolve value conflicts with peers and parents | _____ | _____ |
| Exercises discretion in deciding when to lead and when to follow | _____ | _____ |
| Can complete tasks independently | _____ | _____ |
| Shows satisfaction in completing tasks | _____ | _____ |

In completing this audit, look to your child's attitudes and actions in situations that require the choice of an action or the adoption of a pattern of behavior—managing an allowance, abiding by rules of fair play, helping others, resolving parent-peer conflicts, using free time, completing a project, responding to evaluations in school and/or athletics, etc.

Be realistic. You can't expect as much from a six-year-old as from a ten-year-old. There will always be room for improvement, since these are the years in which skills begin to develop. (You may find it helpful to repeat the audit from time to time to measure progress being made.)

### When Is a Decision Important?

A decision is important when it has special value or meaning for the decider, when it is likely to have impact on others, or when it affects one's prospects for the future. Decisions often produce anxiety and pain when they entail giving up something familiar and moving on to something new and unfamiliar. That's true for everyone, but it can provide particular difficulty for a young child, who will have but limited experience dealing with what's new and unfamiliar.

What may appear unimportant, obvious, or routine to you will often seem completely different to your child.

> Suzanne, a shy child, came home from a scout meeting obviously depressed. The troop she'd recently joined was beginning its annual cookie sale fund-raising drive, and she felt uncomfortable about expectations that she participate. Her parents shrugged off the difficulty she was having, telling her simply not to join in the selling work if it made her uncomfortable. But then, Suzanne protested, the other scout members would think she was not doing her share to support the troop's overall activities.

It's not hard to see that from Suzanne's perspective the situation here involves a confrontation with her insecurities about herself, juxtaposed against a desire to be accepted as a full contributor to a peer group activity. Her parents' failure to see the importance of the decision to her means a lost opportunity for helping her understand how to resolve the dilemma facing her.

Don't be too quick to dismiss a situation that seems easily resolved from your perspective. Whenever your child mentions a problem he or she is having deciding what to do—and especially if it poses a dilemma to him or her—see it as a chance to build decisionmaking skills. Look at the situation and ask yourself

- What is my child trying to work out?
- What approach is he or she following and why?
- Are there better ways to work things through?
- How can I help?

Asking these questions keeps you from jumping to an immediate conclusion that the decision your child faces is unimportant and/or has an obvious solution you can just point out. By keeping alert to problems your child is struggling with, you encourage him or her to turn to you for guidance and support when faced with difficulties, especially insofar as you show yourself sensitive to his or her interests and priorities.

### How to Approach Problems Together

Approach problems with a series of "how to" questions. "How to" questions stimulate your child into developing his or her own alternative responses to troubling circumstances or unexpected opportunities. Each question leads to a set of possibilities, and before you know it, a variety of actions are revealed that are worth considering.

In helping your child through a problem, take time to analyze what the real cause of difficulty is. Only when the underlying cause is clear can an action be developed that makes sense.

Sometimes identifying cause is simple—your child will tell you what it is, or you'll see it clearly on your own. However, as situations become more complex and decisions more important, it's essential to be sure you really have put your finger on the actual cause. Otherwise, you'll work toward a course of action directed at the wrong cause, leaving the real problem unresolved.

The following steps will help you analyze a problem to uncover its cause:

*1.* Determine the discrepancy (difference) between what you and/or your child think *should be* or want and what actually *is.* If there is an unacceptable or uncomfortable difference, there is a problem.

*2.* Try to figure out in specific terms what, where, when, or to what extent there is a discrepancy.

*3.* Identify and compare possible causes.

*4.* Relate the causes you identify to the problem and then select the *most likely* cause.

You begin with recognizing a problem and seeking its cause. Keeping your child's needs and priorities in mind, you help him or her apply the decision framework to developing a response to the cause of the problem; your child learns how to go about making a decision. Your child determines the outcome he or she desires. Your child will explore options (alternatives) and begin to predict and anticipate consequences.

You work through the process together until a course of action is chosen. You take care to both describe and understand the consequences of that action. Then, once the action's been taken, you review the decision's progress and results together. What worked as planned? What went wrong? What adjustments should be made or kept in mind for next time?

### What Is Important to Your Child in General?

Up to the age of twelve (and often beyond), children commonly need help understanding what values are all about. So often they're just vague abstractions. Parents tend to emphasize values without relating them to a child's own feelings and experience. The impression communicated is that values are negatives of some sort—rationales for limits imposed to keep the child under control. There's little effort made to present them as positives, as explanations of what makes certain actions more rewarding than others for the doer.

I've found that both parent and child see a positive focus more clearly when reviewing values in association with experience, particularly when thinking in terms of what has given the child (or parent, for that matter) a sense of accomplishment.

When you have a quiet moment with your child, work through the Pride Chart exercise below. The idea is to chart the degree of pride for each area listed. (You may want to refer to more specific instances in categories indicated or add other categories of your own.)

### Pride Chart

|  | Not Proud | Somewhat Proud | Very Proud |
|---|---|---|---|
| Things you've done for the family | _____ | _____ | _____ |
| Things you've done for a friend | _____ | _____ | _____ |
| Things you've made | _____ | _____ | _____ |
| A skill you've learned | _____ | _____ | _____ |
| How you spend your free time | _____ | _____ | _____ |
| Habits you have | _____ | _____ | _____ |
| How you spend your allowance | _____ | _____ | _____ |
| How you earn extra spending money | _____ | _____ | _____ |
| Performance in school | _____ | _____ | _____ |
| Performance on a team or in a group activity | _____ | _____ | _____ |

The Pride Chart helps your child discover what's important to him or her personally. Your child learns about his or her own values and develops a sharper awareness of what makes some actions more rewarding than others.

You and your child can gain additional benefit if *both* of you complete a Pride Chart and then compare responses. That helps clarify values all around and shows what differences exist. It also aids your child's understanding of why people do different things. (You can extend this activity further by listing things you and/or your child don't like, get mad about, etc.)

## What about Other People?

Considering others is a key element in making important decisions. Unfortunately, it is often a glaring omission in a youngster's choice of action.

Grade school children are selfish and inconsiderate more often than we might like to admit. They are very conscious of the pecking order among their peers and are not above contributing to the bullying of another child in order to keep unwanted attention off themselves. They're still at the stage where a "me first" attitude seems only natural.

It takes constant reminding at this stage in a child's life to build an awareness of how others are affected by a decision. Fortunately, there are many daily events that provide occasion for getting your child to think about others.

> Ten-year-old Darrell continually rebuffed his six-year-old brother Robbie's efforts to join in games or activities with him. When his parents remarked on this behavior, he responded that Robbie was too little to fit into his activities and that he shouldn't have to include him. His parents asked Darrell if this conclusion should also apply to activities Darrell enjoyed sharing with them. He admitted he didn't want that kind of standard applied to him. After further discussion, he agreed to make more effort to include Robbie in some of his activities. His parents in turn pointed out to Robbie that Darrell couldn't be expected to include him in all activities and advised the two boys to work out some agreement on what activities they would share and when.

Darrell and Robbie's parents are using empathy to build Darrell's awareness of his younger brother's feelings, asking Darrell to imagine himself in the kind of situation he puts Robbie in.

It's easy to promote consideration for others in your child. Set a clear example. When it comes to a family decision, give everyone the chance to express his or her viewpoint while the others listen. Discuss how you see your decisions affecting other people and how that in turn affects what you decide to do. Encourage your child to do the same. Ask your child to imagine the effect of something he or she might do on someone else. How does your child think a friend might behave in a given circumstance involving him or her or another friend? What does your child observe about people's reactions to what others do; for example, at a party or in an incident at school?

Your efforts here aim at getting your child to be sensitive to another person's position before taking action—to see that there can be an effect on someone and to take that effect into account when deciding to act. Remember that building awareness here will take some time. Your grade school child will need a lot of guidance and reminding before the effect on other people figures as an automatic consideration in every decision made.

## What Response to the World Beyond Home?

All kinds of differences become apparent to your child as peer groups become more important and as new rules are established in school or other settings outside the home. Your child has to respond to other adults who may in certain circumstances seem to have more authority and power than his or her parents.

Your child will inevitably discover that decisions can't always be made according to the rules or philosophy of the home. Sometimes they will provide no guidance because the situation at hand is totally new. Sometimes they will require adjustment because relationships outside the home are not the same as relationships inside the home.

It's through developing some sense of the outside world and what is likely to be encountered there that your child learns what adjustments to make. Active involvement in the world outside the home stimulates awareness here. Any number of activities lend themselves to this—anything from playing on a Little League team to singing in a choir to having a paper route.

> Sylvia took over her older brother's newspaper delivery route after he'd become involved in other activities. She soon expressed frustration with difficulty she was having collecting money due from two of her customers. She felt uncomfortable pressing adults for money owed her. The family philosophy consistently emphasized respect for adults inside and outside the home. Her parents pointed out that persistence in efforts to get the money due her was a necessary condition to taking on the responsibility of the route. They then helped her work out and rehearse "reminders" to her customers who had overdue accounts.

Activities inside the home can build awareness of the outside world as well. Examples would be watching TV news together, discussing a local or national event your child can relate to, and sharing what each family member's out-of-home experiences during the day have been. In each case, the object remains to expose your child to the reality of differences in such a way as to foster insight into why people do certain things.

One good starting point is getting your child to describe friends and schoolmates who live by different rules. Discuss these differences. Have your child play out the implications of living by different rules and according to different routines. Use whatever chance you can to get your child to see and understand the why's and do's and don't's of the world beyond the home.

### What Should Happen If . . . ?

By now your child already knows the limits established in the home and the consequences attached to these. And now he or she is ready to discuss and help formulate them.

You'll find your child has excellent ideas about consequences by the age of nine or ten—perhaps even before then. After a couple of years of school and broadened experience with the consequences used in other families, your child has a good perspective on what makes sense and what doesn't in most everyday situations.

Include all of your children when formulating or adjusting elements of the family philosophy. After all, the guidelines apply to them, too, so it's logical they should have something to say about them.

An easy way to begin to involve a child in defining/revising limits and consequences is to work out a list of situations he or she can imagine him- or herself in (not that he or she necessarily ever will be). A sample list might go something like this:

| *What should happen if...?* | *Suggested consequence* |
| --- | --- |
| You came home late? | _____ |
| You fail a subject? | _____ |
| You don't get to school on time? | _____ |
| Your room is not kept picked up? | _____ |
| You cheat on a test? | _____ |
| Your homework is not completed? | _____ |
| You hit your brother? | _____ |
| You lose your watch? | _____ |
| You talk back? | _____ |
| Your tasks around the house are not completed? | _____ |

Discuss the suggestions, then make up a list of consequences everyone is willing to live by. (Look back to the guidelines set out in Chapter 11 to help ensure the consequences established fit the situation.) Invite your child to make additions that involve your behavior as well.

Don't leave it at a negative focus, however. Make a list of positive consequences, too. For example, what should happen if ... you complete jobs around the house faithfully?... improve your grades?. . . keep your room in good order? (And, again, try to establish consequences that relate directly to the behavior demonstrated.)

Developing these lists jointly with your child increases awareness for both of you. In addition, joint involvement virtually always leads to a heightened sense of commitment, resulting in more responsible behavior.

### THE FAMILY MEETING

Your grade school child very naturally feels his or her point of view merits consideration when it come to the routines, limits, and consequences he or she is expected to adhere to. That should neither surprise you nor upset you. As we've seen, building decision skills entails promoting your child's recognition of what goes into a choice of action. In the family setting, that includes involving your child in decisions that affect him or her as a family member with unique interests and priorities.

In my experience, nothing does more to promote involvement in and commitment to decisions made about the family than the institution of regular family meetings in which everyone participates.

Family meetings provide everyone an opportunity to have a say about situations that affect them as members of the family. They give everyone a chance to explain or question values, to define or question goals, to suggest alternative lines of action. They provide everyone an increased information flow, promote a more complete view of risks and consequences attached to any action, and ensure that everyone understands clearly the what and why of decisions made. The family meeting also provides an ideal forum for reviewing decisions made and actions taken.

Greg's parents found it difficult to accept Paul, a friend Greg spent much of his free time with. They had evidence that Paul was reckless and irresponsible in many of his actions. However, while convinced Paul could have a negative impact on Greg, they were reluctant to forbid contact with him, as they sensed Greg would react with resentment at this exercise of parental authority, perhaps adopting secretive behavior to keep up his friendship with Paul.

They voiced their concern about Paul in a family meeting, pointing out specific indications they had of behavior they felt was unacceptable. At the same time, they reassured Greg that they did not wish to regulate his friendships for him. In the family meeting, Greg's parents, Greg himself, and Greg's younger sister worked out guidelines Greg could apply in his relations with Paul and agreed on consequences that would apply if the limits contained in those guidelines were violated. Greg's sister suggested the parents also tell Paul directly of concerns about his behavior the next time a good opportunity for that arose.

Family meetings are particularly useful for developing an approach to problems facing or involving your child. They make possible your expressing concern without that immediately being seen as an effort to unilaterally impose your solutions. Since your child is directly involved in decisions about solutions, you're more assured that he or she will follow through in an appropriate fashion.

### Family Meeting Guidelines

To obtain the maximum benefit from family meetings, observe these simple guidelines:

*1. Schedule meetings on a regular basis.* Work out a time when everyone is at home. Make it clear that the family meeting is a priority event and that everyone—parents and children—is expected to attend. Any rescheduling required by unavoidable conflict with other activities must be with the consent of all family members.

How often should you have meetings? You may opt for holding them once a week. I recommend meeting at least twice a month.

2. *Set up a minimal agenda of things to discuss and review each time.* That way meetings will get to the point quickly. You won't find yourself and/or other family members sitting around unsure of what to say or how to introduce something for everyone's consideration.

A sample agenda might be:

A review of events/decisions made over the past week affecting the family

New developments requiring response, either planning future actions or adjusting present routines and family policies

Problems involving or existing between family members

3. *Make sure everyone participates equally.* A family meeting should not be used as an occasion for parents to impose their priorities and choices while children do little more than take note of what's expected of them. The point is to involve your children totally, so that decisions reached are theirs as well as yours. That means:

- Your child has the same freedom as you have to introduce a subject or question for discussion.
- Your child has the same freedom to question or comment on others' views and behavior and to explain or defend his or her own.
- You listen as attentively and respectfully to your child as you expect him or her to listen to you.
- You show the same concern to win your child's understanding of and concurrence in decisions made as you expect others to show you.

4. *Work to establish a consensus among family members on decisions made.* Again, the point is to involve your child in the process and to win his or her concurrence in decisions that apply to him or her. Obviously reality has to be taken into account—you can't allow a family member to filibuster so that

a needed action is totally blocked. However, don't short-circuit your child's efforts to have his or her say with a repeated excuse that circumstances require things being done your way immediately. If there is an immediate need for action, point to that and work for a quick decision, but one that allows your child a chance to be heard.

You will at times find yourself dealing with problem situations that require disciplinary measures. In that case, of course, your actions will depend on an understanding of limits and consequences already established; you're not going to approach this kind of situation as one presenting new choices that excuse behavior already defined as unacceptable. So then you'll be reviewing behavior and explaining an action taken or to be taken that does not require your child's concurrence at this point. But this should happen only where limits have already been defined clearly and where it's obvious to all that those limits have been exceeded. Anything that requires defining new limits or adjusting old ones should be approached on a consensus basis.

5. *Keep your meetings comfortably brief.* You don't want family meetings to turn into marathon sessions that everybody comes to dread. In particular, you want to avoid meetings characterized by argument and efforts on the part of either parents or child to have the last word. You'll find it helpful to review Chapter 9, "Managing Differences," and the communication guidelines set out in Chapter 10 to keep things on track here. My experience is that most family meetings can be satisfactorily conducted in fifteen to twenty minutes.

6. *Give every family member the option to call special meetings when necessary.* Decision situations don't arise according to some neat schedule. Something can come up at any time that affects the family. A family member may encounter a problem that needs immediate attention. Decide together what circumstances warrant calling special meetings and how everyone will be notified. Once the circumstances have been spelled

out, your child should have as much right to call for a special meeting as you have. He or she shouldn't need special permission from you to do so.

Follow the same guidelines in the conduct of special meetings as with regular meetings.

There's great scope for involving children of grade school age in family decisions, and you can do a lot to stimulate their developing sound decisionmaking skills to apply on their own. It's surprising sometimes how capably a child of ten or eleven can handle private affairs once he or she is attuned to the considerations attached to taking action.

But let me repeat an earlier note of caution. While you can reasonably expect a grade school child to develop and demonstrate awareness and skills in making decisions, it's not reasonable to expect the same level of awareness and skill that you've achieved. There will be failures, some due to inadvertent error, others due to impatience, and still others due to impulsive or "me first" behavior your child has not yet outgrown. And because your child's experience of things over a long term is still very limited, short-term considerations will frequently be accorded precedence over long-term considerations.

You'll help your child best if in all your efforts you keep his or her limitations in mind and exercise patience when it comes to expectations about results.

# 14

# The "Don't Bug Me!" Years —Junior High

Your child begins making decisions on his or her own by the start of grade school. However, it isn't until about the time your child reaches junior high that it's obvious how crucial *his or her* decisions are.

The junior high years are perhaps the most critical period in life planning and decisionmaking. It's now that your child begins developing a sense of his or her own place in the world. Yes, your child has been doing that all along, but a change is in process now. Previously your child included home and family as natural, even primary components of his or her world. Now your child begins to go beyond home and family in a new way, as points of focus to put behind him or her. The difficulty is that your child is still some years from actually doing so, and considerable tensions can (and do) build up in the meantime.

The junior high years find the young adolescent struggling for independence while trying to figure out how to fit into the general scheme of things. Peer pressure becomes particularly intense and contributes to conflict in the family. Your child feels ready to be treated as a grownup, but feels an equally strong need to be liked and accepted by his or her peers. A contradiction develops. While independence is a main concern, frequently an almost mindless conformity to peer expectations develops, which you as a parent see as the very antithesis of maturity.

At this stage, your child's decisions, whether actively or passively made—that is, whether made on his or her own or amounting to going along with the group—tend to revolve about roles and stereotypes. Junior high children get caught up in who is (or whether they themselves are) "preppy," "brainy," "a jock," "a greaser," "straight," or whatever contemporary label seems to fit their appearance and disposition. And there's a great tendency to act these roles or labels out completely.

At perhaps no other time must a parent be more on the ball than when it comes to managing differences and helping with decisions. This is no mean task, however, because the young adolescent, seeing new experiences within reach for the first time and associating them with independence, tends to reach for those with little sense of the long-term implications involved. Behavior is often directed more toward immediate self-gratification and self-assertion than to interests beyond the moment. Just when you think a capacity for planning over the long term should be coming into play, your child's impatience to decide things according to his or her own immediate whims threatens to complicate matters.

### THE DILEMMA FOR PARENTS

Junior high students face decision situations with potentially severe consequences. Look at the range of possibilities:

- Choosing a course of study
- Meeting school responsibilities
- Considering future occupations
- Joining in unsupervised peer activities
- Selecting leisure activities
- Following adult rules
- Obeying the law
- Managing money

- Working part-time
- Relating to the opposite sex
- Setting personal standards of dress and appearance
- Dealing with temptations like alcohol or drug use

Parents have every reason to feel uneasy at this time. But all too often they take a counterproductive approach to heading off the problems they're concerned about. They revert to a telling approach, when what's really needed is careful guidance that shows the child how to head off problems on his or her own.

In these years, your particular task is to pay special attention to the importance of planning, developing an ever more certain awareness of consequences so that your child comes to recognize the pitfalls in decisions made too hastily and for the wrong reasons. You must help your child see that the wrong reasons have to do with the impact of an action upon him- or herself. It isn't—or shouldn't be—primarily a question of whether or not you approve. At the same time, knowing your child must now begin to prepare for life-shaping decisions in the near future, you must concentrate on building a positive self-image, so your child begins to feel strong enough to act independently.

Always keep the limitations and biases of your own perspective in mind. As in previous years, what may appear unimportant, obvious, or routine to you may not appear that way to your child, and with good reason. When, for example, you know your youngster is eager to have a better social life, the decision to attend a class dance seems logical and easy. It may not be so at all. In his or her world, this may be a tremendous venture in which he or she risks self-esteem and jeopardizing relations with peers.

To be of help, you have to have insight into how your child sees and makes decisions. Even if you think you already have that, it's best to double-check. The changes a child goes through in adolescence sometimes seem so many and so overwhelming that he or she finds it easier to shortcut the decision process than to follow it through. That can lead to real disaster. It will help if you can find some way to keep your child's attention on the reality that good decisions do provide benefits he or she genuinely wants for him- or herself.

### Evaluating Decisions Made

You can help your child here simply through informal discussions—listening to problems he or she is facing, exchanging ideas about possible action to take, talking about results.

I've also found it helpful to ask adolescents to keep a record of decisions they make. Have your child identify important decisions made over a period of weeks, then have him or her track what happened with those. (I've provided a chart you can adapt to simplify doing this.)

Getting your child to chart a series of decisions will help him or her a lot. Your child will tune into what he or she is doing more readily. Your child will see what happens as a result of following his or her own priorities. Your child will see what happens when giving in to pressures from others. Your child will learn to consider results along a continuum—that results develop over time; that they don't all immediately come to pass. If your child often feels dissatisfaction with how things turn out, he or she will get some idea of what specifically contributes to that. Just as important, your child will also see what he or she has been doing right more clearly.

You may doubt your child's readiness to follow through with this exercise. Junior high students frequently resent parental guidance—they see it as interference—and shun advice. But you must remain involved. Behavior in these years shapes later life, even decisions that seem to relate only to what's happening now.

Getting your child to do this is easier if you agree to chart your own decisions at the same time. Then it doesn't seem so much an imposed activity—one of those parent-devised tests he or she is supposed to pass. Then it becomes more a mutual

## What Happens with My Important Decisions?

| Decision | My priorities (values and goals) | Pressures | | Information relied on | | Action | Results |
|---|---|---|---|---|---|---|---|
| | | Family | Friends | From others | What I knew/found out | | |
| 1. | | | | | | | |
| 2. | | | | | | | |
| 3. | | | | | | | |
| 4. | | | | | | | |
| 5. | | | | | | | |

## How Do I Feel about the Results?

| | At first | 1 week later | 2 weeks later | 1 month later |
|---|---|---|---|---|
| 1. | | | | |
| 2. | | | | |
| 3. | | | | |
| 4. | | | | |
| 5. | | | | |

help situation. You can compare the patterns that emerge; you can both make suggestions.

When sharing this activity, don't assume your chart has to be better than your child's—that you have to provide a perfect example. In truth, your child will find it easier to accept a need for adjustment of his or her own perspectives and actions through seeing that you have to do the same from time to time. Making this a shared experience can do a lot to show your child that adult life requires a coherent line of approach and periodic adjustments, too. Your child will see the decision framework isn't simply something he or she is obliged to follow because he or she isn't deemed sufficiently mature to do things in his or her own way.

Work out an agreement with your child about which decision areas to chart. Insisting your child chart them all may be interpreted as an effort on your part to pry into all his or her personal affairs. The point is to cue your child into making good decisions, not to lay everything out for your review and approval. You child will read that as interference, not guidance.

> Tracy and her mother agreed to review their respective approaches to decision situations that faced each of them regularly. After some discussion, they decided to chart decisions in the areas of social activity and family interactions. Once a week for a month they'd compare charts and discuss patterns evident in them. Both agreed that these discussions would focus on developing a positive approach to situations. Both agreed that either could call a "time out" on discussions should these lead to argument or judgmental criticism from the other.

Of course you won't always agree with each other's priorities. You may feel that the response to pressures exerted by others is inappropriate or that not enough has been done to examine alternatives. Should you just stifle those reactions? Should you hold back from introducing for consideration alternatives you think should have been taken into consideration?

No. The whole point of discussion is to have an exchange of

views. You *can* identify and explain differences in how you might have approached a decision facing your child. That's how children learn to see beyond the limits of their own point of view. Just be sure to keep the line of communication open on a two-way basis. Ask questions in preference to making dogmatic assertions—"What do you think might have happened if you'd taken this course of action?" rather than "You should have done it this way!" Make suggestions, don't give orders. (It will help you to review Chapter 9 and Chapter 10 in connection with this activity.)

### WHAT ABOUT PROBLEMS?

It's all very fine to take a positive approach, you may be thinking, but let's be realistic. This is a problem age. Even under the best of circumstances, you know you're going to have to deal with problems, and these will include some beauts.

> Philip, a seventh grader, asked his mother for help. "All my friends are smoking. They make fun of me for not doing it. It's getting tough to say 'no.'"

What does a father or mother say?

A lot of them say something along the lines of "If I find out about it, you're in big trouble." And then, in another place and another time, a "friend" looks your child in the eye and sneers, "Oh, your old man/lady . . . !" Then, just to prove your child is not your puppet—just to prove to everyone, and particularly to him- or herself, that he or she makes his or her own decisions—your child makes the decision that puts him or her in "big trouble."

Your adolescent child is at the age when independence is naturally a priority value. You may be able to control that with an "I'm telling you" approach to things, but you'll get doubtful results if you do. If your attempt succeeds, you only program your child into a dependence on others to make decisions for him or her. If your attempt fails, it'll fail in conflict, with you distancing yourself from your child.

> Philip's mother expressed surprise, then stopped what she was doing. "I know that's a very important decision for you. It sounds like you want to say 'no' but don't quite know how without seeming square or chicken. Would you like some ideas from me now? I can think of some ways you might want to handle this. Do you want us to call a special family meeting?"

Parents underestimate their children sometimes. Often a child will know what he or she really wants to do, if only people would leave him or her alone. What your child wants is often actually in line with family background and upbringing. In asking for help, your child is not necessarily asking you to supply any answers; he or she is asking for support in piecing together and following through on his or her own decision.

But suppose your child is hoping you'll tell him or her what to do? Well, think about it. Don't you ultimately hope to see him or her up to the important decisions everyone faces in life? Isn't your child better off learning how to make those for him- or herself?

Provide support. Agree on limits to be observed. Share your experience and feelings. Make suggestions that will help your child decide. Keep an eye on actions and results so you know when intervention may be necessary (when things are clearly beyond your child's control; when your child is clearly in danger). You can do all of that—and it can make a world of difference—without taking over your child's life. Think of yourself as something of a coach. You can prepare the player for the game ahead, but you can't play and win it for him or her.

### Agree on Limits?

It's difficult for many parents to imagine agreeing on limits with an adolescent. A child this age doesn't want to know from limits, it seems. You feel you have to tell your child what you expect of him or her and rely on your authority to make the point stick. If adolescents won't listen to you half the time, how can you expect them to agree to rules they are going to have to follow?

It isn't always easy. But the alternative isn't any better— telling a twelve- or thirteen-year-old what to do doesn't work either, as often as not. It puts you up against that powerful drive toward independence we just noted.

> Miriam, precociously developed at age twelve, was cutting school to hang out with a group of teenagers who focused most of their energies on idle amusement and cultivating a "punk" life-style. Her mother, a harried single parent, berated and threatened her time and again, even cut off Miriam's allowance, the only consequence she felt capable of enforcing. Things got no better. In desperation, she sought counseling assistance. The counselor helped her see that her efforts to force her child into approved behavior had only resulted in a communication barrier. What was essential now was reestablishing some kind of positive relationship to rebuild influence she had lost with her daughter.

Keeping lines of communication open is essential. When you have a breakdown there, you can all too easily find yourself in desperate straits. By relying on a negative approach to behavior—one that concentrates on "don't's"—you risk negative results. Your adolescent is very apt to tune you out and prove his or her independence by doing the exact opposite of what you want.

I've found two devices of immense value during the adolescent and teen years: the family meeting and negotiated goal contracts.

As you'll recall, the family meeting involves your child as a full participant in family decisions, including those on limits and consequences. It provides a forum in which feelings can be aired and opinions exchanged on a regular basis. It allows everyone opportunity to discuss problems they're having or difficulties they see in the behavior of others. In addition, it gives everyone a chance to share good feelings—about accomplishments, about relationships within or outside the family. (Look back to Chapter 13 for guidelines on conducting family meetings. Again, it will also help to review Chapter 9 and the communication section of Chapter 10.)

> The counselor got Miriam and her mother both to agree to set aside a regular time for exchanging feelings and discussing them on a person-to-person basis. He coached them through several practice sessions. He got both to agree to put at least equal focus on good feelings—about themselves, about each other, about friends, etc.—without either undercutting that through responding with criticism or negative judgments. Although communication difficulties still occasionally arose, in two months' time Miriam and her mother found themselves talking things over more openly. Miriam's behavior became less of a problem.

Even if there are only two of you and you're in each other's company every day, it pays to schedule special times to exchange viewpoints and feelings. Now more than ever it's important you work out a shared family philosophy, one parent(s) and child explicitly accept. Disagreements will arise, of course, even in the best of situations. Airing those openly with an eye toward accommodating differences in line with the family philosophy will help keep things manageable.

In connection with all this, keep positive consequences in mind for encouraging responsible behavior. There are lots of things you can offer and/or share with an adolescent child that he or she can't easily get or do without you. Go out to a play or concert together; go to a favorite sporting event; encourage him or her to invite a friend over for dinner or to share a family trip with you. Work out a goal contract that sets up a positive consequence for positive achievement.

Yes, you may be saying, but sometimes even these points of attention won't ensure agreement between parent and child when it comes to behavior problems. Sometimes you just have to lay down the law.

> The principal at Eliot's junior high school called his parents in for an emergency conference. She informed them that Eliot and

several others had stolen more than $70 from a teacher's pocketbook. Eliot was caught dividing the take with his cohorts in the boys' restroom. The principal told Eliot's parents that she was suspending him from school for a week and that she hoped they would follow through with appropriate disciplinary action.

Okay, what do Eliot's parents do? Get his agreement to whatever disciplinary measures they take?

Stealing, whether it's taking candy from a store, shoplifting, taking change from your pocket or purse, or taking another person's property, is fairly common in the late elementary and junior high years. It's very embarrassing for the parents. It reflects on the whole family and sparks quick and intense anger. What usually happens is that the parents pay for the loss to show they care about what happened and discipline their child to emphasize their feelings about stealing.

What about Eliot's situation? He didn't steal out of need. Maybe he was trying to buy friends or win peer recognition. His parents would do well to look for the cause of his behavior. Ultimately their actions should help Eliot deal with that cause; the disciplinary consequences imposed should tie in with that cause somehow.

Eliot's parents reminded him of a basic principle of the family philosophy he had always agreed with—the Golden Rule: Do unto others as you would have them do unto you. They asked him to imagine how he would feel if someone stole his week's allowance from him. Eliot admitted he would be angry. They asked him what he would think appropriate discipline for someone who stole from him. He admitted he'd probably want something more than just to get his money back, something that would show the other person was aware he'd done something wrong. Why had Eliot taken the money? He haltingly confessed he'd done it on a dare, to see if he had the nerve. He agreed a personal apology was in order. His parents also pointed out that a curfew restriction was in order, in line with previously agreed-to consequences to be applied in the event of serious misbehavior outside the home.

Winning your child's agreement in this kind of situation isn't a question of giving him or her veto power over any consequence to be applied for misbehavior. It's a matter of making connections he or she sees as valid—connections with the family philosophy, connections about how others are affected by his or her actions, and connections with values your child personally subscribes to as a rule.

Draw those connections. Have your child verify his or her understanding of them. Ask your child to consider the situation from the perspective of someone affected by his or her action; refer to your child's own part in establishing and subscribing to relevant points of the family philosophy. Then follow through with a consequence your child can see ties in with what happened. (Eliot's parents, for example, could emphasize that taking responsibility for mistakes is a better measure of nerve than giving in to pressure to go along with the crowd.) You don't have to put it up for a vote requiring unanimous consent at this point. Clearly drawing the connections to what your child has already acknowledged and agreed to is enough.

It's in an example like this that you see how important a family philosophy is. Look back to Chapter 10 again for assistance if you're not sure you've established one in your family that everyone recognizes and agrees to. Don't wait until things go wrong to try to get agreement on values to uphold and general goals to aim for.

Of course you can't anticipate everything. But keep in mind that there are broadly expressed behavioral principles that apply naturally in many situations. The Golden Rule is perhaps the best example, a principle easily understood and agreed to, covering problems arising out of lack of consideration for others—dishonesty, belligerence, indifference, thoughtlessness. Establishing even a few basic principles as *shared* standards of conduct will influence behavior in positive directions. It will also make it easier to apply consequences that clearly relate to the action and that your child has already accepted as appropriate.

**BUILDING SKILLS**

There will be problems to deal with, but don't make the mistake of concentrating just on coping with problems. The more basic task is building skills. You want your child to be able to handle opportunities, too. You want to help set him or her on a course that leads to achievement—responsible independence at the least—not one that merely keeps your child out of trouble.

The main point of concern in this connection is discovering what is important enough to commit to in future actions. This discovery makes possible a transition from adult-directed behavior to independent action taken with awareness and self-confidence.

Four basic skills should be emphasized in this transition period:

*1.* Translating values into goals
*2.* Clarifying and pursuing what is wanted (goals)
*3.* Discovering and developing ways to reach goals
*4.* Learning to assess the risks (consequences) involved in any action

Get a sense of what your child feels is important to him or her now. That's where you start—it's a continuation of what you've done before. But now add in a further dimension: What does your child see as important to him or her in years to come? You can determine this in discussion with your child. It may help to employ the exercise below.

**What Do I Think Is Important?**

| At the age I am now: | Most important | Somewhat important | Least important |
|---|---|---|---|
| 1. Get along with friends and be popular | _____ | _____ | _____ |
| 2. Have nice clothes | _____ | _____ | _____ |
| 3. Be a good student | _____ | _____ | _____ |

| At the age I am now: | Most important | Somewhat important | Least important |
|---|---|---|---|
| 4. Accomplish what my parents expect | _____ | _____ | _____ |
| 5. Be a good athlete | _____ | _____ | _____ |
| 6. Be independent | _____ | _____ | _____ |
| 7. Work for my own future | _____ | _____ | _____ |

*In the future:*

| | Most important | Somewhat important | Least important |
|---|---|---|---|
| 1. Make a name for myself in my career | _____ | _____ | _____ |
| 2. Contribute to society | _____ | _____ | _____ |
| 3. Get along with friends and be popular | _____ | _____ | _____ |
| 4. Make lots of money so I can have the things I want | _____ | _____ | _____ |
| 5. Get married and have a nice family | _____ | _____ | _____ |
| 6. Express myself in some creative way | _____ | _____ | _____ |
| 7. Be independent | _____ | _____ | _____ |
| 8. Have a goal or commitment for my life | _____ | _____ | _____ |
| 9. Have free time to myself | _____ | _____ | _____ |
| 10. Follow my religious beliefs | _____ | _____ | _____ |

Knowing what's important to your child is critical in the junior high transition period, for both of you. Pushing off into the future—and providing appropriate support—requires an accurate picture of priorities. Movement toward anything hinges on your child's need and readiness to pursue those priorities, anticipating an adequate payoff for any action taken.

### Translating Values into Goals

How is it possible to have one child who studies and another of equal ability who doesn't? What makes it routine for one child to plan ahead while another can't seem to make it through the day? Why does one child have no difficulty saying no to friends while another finds it impossible to resist peer pressures?

The difference in what is important and why will explain some of the differences in behavior, but there's more involved than just knowing what's important. One also has to know how to translate what's important into specific objectives to aim for. If you haven't drawn some connection between what's important and what you can do about it, you're likely to do nothing that has any particular focus.

Confusion, apparent lack of motivation, and an "I couldn't care less" attitude are common characteristics of junior high children. The youngster who can't be moved or motivated by anything is probably telling you: "I don't see much value in anything. How do you expect me to get going when I don't know what to aim for?"

This doesn't boil down to a question of ability. Most youngsters at this age have the capability for deciding and taking action in a well-considered manner. They have trouble because they haven't developed that capability. They need help putting it to work for them, so they see that the positive returns of accomplishing something are within reach.

You don't have to start with ambitious projects. It's more important to build a record of modest successes, which will develop confidence and increase motivation for continued decisive action. There's a risk in starting with plans on a major scale: Failure at any point may prove so discouraging that the decisionmaking technique itself is drawn into question, even though the technique is not at fault. Minor setbacks are less problematic. Your child is more likely to see them as a challenge than as a repudiation, and he or she will more readily refer to the decision framework again for deciding on adjustments and new lines of approach.

There are several possible difficulties to be alert to in getting your child to set meaningful goals for him- or herself.

*1.* Sometimes your child will go after a goal without knowing the real payoff or return. He or she will be on something of a fantasy trip relative to what the goal means, and not recognize that it introduces a world of consequences and considerations he or she hasn't begun to take into account.

*2.* Sometimes your child won't really be sure whether he or she is going after something he or she wants or after something somebody else wants for him or her.

*3.* Sometimes your child will not anticipate peer pressure to do something out of line with his or her own priorities.

*4.* Sometimes your child will underestimate the resources required to make progress toward a goal.

Most problems here arise from making a misconnection between what your child thinks is important and what will provide a concrete payoff in line with that.

> Moira envied two other girls in her class their evident popularity with the other students. Both girls came from families with good income. They were always very well dressed and had the benefit of regular visits to a top-rated local beauty salon. Moira became obsessed with demonstrating her own good taste in clothes and cosmetics and increasingly hounded her parents to provide her an expensive wardrobe and money for beauty appointments. When they pointed out that they could not easily afford to provide her these things, Moira became angry and accused them of not caring about how others in her class respected her.

Moira has made a misconnection along the lines of problem 1 above. She's setting herself an appearance-related goal, thinking that will provide her what is really a personality-related benefit. What her parents need to help her do in this situation is make the appropriate connection for getting what she really wants.

Children often need help in drawing realistic connections between what's important to them and what action to take to achieve the appropriate value payoff. Parents can help by getting them to consider what they do in all contexts more attentively, particularly with regard to value payoffs. Keeping a decision chart will help sharpen awareness of value payoffs gained or missed because of choices made.

Your child may also benefit from keeping an activity log over the space of a week or two to note what activities absorb what percentage of his or her time and what value payoffs each provides. A simple form like the one below will do. Have your child note how his or her time was spent—doing homework, playing on a team, doing assigned chores, reading, watching TV, sharing time with people, spending time alone, etc. Then have your child review that to pull out the things that seem important to him or her. Point out that time spent on an activity is often a measure of importance. What does your child spend a lot of time doing? Why? What value tie-in does he or she see?

### Sample Log Format

|  | Mon. | Tues. | Wed. | Thurs. | Fri. | Sat. | Sun. |
|---|---|---|---|---|---|---|---|
| Before school (or morning) |  |  |  |  |  |  |  |
| After school (or afternoon) |  |  |  |  |  |  |  |
| Evenings |  |  |  |  |  |  |  |

This exercise is particularly useful: It gets children to see that daily activity is decision-determined, too. Young people sometimes think of decisions as special events—like deciding what course of study to take, whom to ask to a dance, what present to buy a special friend. They don't stop to think that everyday routines aim at value payoffs, too.

Lonnie told his parents he resented the amount of time his household chores took him. They kept him from doing things he would rather do that he felt he would get much more out of. He particularly resented giving up so much of his weekend time, when other friends were out together playing basketball.

Unless they are given certain responsibilities, youngsters will tend to do what they want. They'll generally avoid anything that entails an uncomfortable effort unless there's an obvious compensating payoff to be gained from it. A budding athlete, for example, who puts in long, hard hours of training in anticipation of a victory that brings recognition and acclaim, may protest mightily at some routine home task that is his or her responsibility. Your child doesn't see that he or she gets anything out of that.

> Lonnie's parents told him they were not ready to relieve him of the responsibilities that were his. The family philosophy clearly stated that everyone had a share in maintaining a family environment that all found enjoyable. They suggested that he take an alternative approach to his chores, perhaps devoting some time to them every day after school so that he'd have more free weekend time.

Here again the family philosophy can point the way. It provides a framework within which the family's affairs are conducted. It points to values that the family lives by on a day-to-day basis, values that youngsters sometimes lose track of because they so readily start to take things for granted.

Goal contracts can also help here. If your child finds it difficult to accept routine responsibilities, draw up a contract that points to a value payoff he or she can look forward to. Try to relate that payoff to the payoff that the resented task actually provides. For example, sharing tasks around the house provides everyone guaranteed free time. Draw up a goal contract in which you promise an independent or shared family activity your youngster will look forward to in exchange for his or her accepting assigned responsibilities without complaint.

Don't underestimate the power of simple positive reinforcement. Adolescents respond to recognition and encouragement, too. They like being told their work is appreciated. They generally respond with effort when it's clear others are prepared to acknowledge that. In seeing the appreciation others have for a job well done, they are prompted into a more ready appreciation of their own for a job well done. They'll start to tune into value payoffs in everyday routines. They'll get a more realistic sense of the connections between their actions and what's important to them in their day-to-day existence.

Use your family meeting to ease the way.

> Conrad complained continually about having to do yardwork. His parents, weary of his whining protestations, finally brought this up at a family meeting. After some discussion, all agreed to draw up a list of tasks around the home that required doing on a regular basis, indicating the amount of time each task took during an average week. They also made note of the benefits each task provided. Then at a special family meeting held the following week, family members reviewed the division of responsibilities. Conrad agreed with the others that fairness entails sharing responsibility. His parents agreed to negotiate specific responsibilities, provided that the general rule of shared responsibility was followed. In reviewing the list of chores to select from at the next meeting, Conrad decided that he would rather stick with the yardwork than take on other necessary chores in a trade-off.

### Clarifying and Pursuing What Is Wanted

As soon as you make a statement about wanting something, you're projecting yourself into the future—looking toward a time when you have that something. That means planning.

Planning begins with identifying something as being worth going after. It requires establishing a focus. Adolescents often have trouble here because they haven't yet developed a sense of direction about what they want. They identify goals without understanding what those really are or entail by way of action.

While it may be difficult to get a junior high student to sit down and apply thought to goals he or she thinks are already clear, your child will benefit from doing so. A good way to go about it is to make some of the following activities family endeavors. Everyone will benefit.

Choose an appropriate time to meet as a group to establish goals for the coming year. (They need not require the entire year to complete.) Post the various goal statements, and have family members check them off when completed or post revisions as necessary. Revisions should depend on new information coming to light or a change in circumstances, either of which should be explained. The idea is to develop clear goals and to share experiences relating to difficulties encountered along the way.

Check each goal statement for clarity before posting it. The clarity requirement will be met if the statement specifies:

*1.* What the person will have or be able to do once the goal is reached;

*2.* What time schedule or time limits have been set;

*3.* How the goal setter will know when the goal has been reached.

A good way to help your youngster here is to have him or her focus on things he or she would like to see improve within the time frame adopted. (That's a good approach for you, too, if you find it less easy to formulate goals than you expected.) Here's an example of how your child might do this:

### Self-Improvement Goals

| Things I'd like to do better | Description | Goal | Things I have to do |
|---|---|---|---|
| Schoolwork | _____ | _____ | _____ |
| Getting along with people | _____ | _____ | _____ |
| Sports/leisure activities | _____ | _____ | _____ |
| Managing my finances | _____ | _____ | _____ |
| Having more friends | _____ | _____ | _____ |
| Feeling more confident and satisfied with myself | _____ | _____ | _____ |
| Knowing what I want in the future | _____ | _____ | _____ |

The first column is basically a category listing—the broad focus, which your child can usually manage fairly easily. The description column narrows that focus by stating what the specifics are to work on. The goal column sets out how the specifics are to change. The final column is the action column.

This fairly simple approach will automatically prompt consideration of the questions that have to be answered if a plan of action is to prove effective: Are my goals realistic? Which goal is most important to me? What makes going after these goals worth the effort? Your child has to assess his or her strengths and weaknesses consciously, set value priorities, and anticipate obstacles.

Some typical goals among junior high groups I've worked with have been:

- I want to make two new friends this semester.
- I want to save $200 by the end of the year to buy a bike.
- I want to take a course to learn about auto mechanics.
- I want to earn all my own spending money.
- I want to be elected to a class office.
- I want recognition from my parents for doing something well.

Establishing, clarifying, and pursuing goals usually require parental assistance. Get involved with your child's pursuits. Share your own struggles to reach your goals; talk about your feelings of frustration and satisfaction as you suffer setbacks and make gains along the way. Remember, your child must see that what you're asking him or her to do is to develop a mature approach to making decisions. It's not another case of having to do something because he or she is a child who doesn't know better.

### Discovering and Developing Ways to Reach Goals

When you're twelve or fourteen, it is difficult to see all the possibilities for response to a situation. Often it seems a lot easier to go with the "obvious" than to do some independent thinking. That's easier, at least in the short run, because all a youngster has to do is check out what "everybody else" is doing.

Over the long term, this leads to trouble. For one thing, your child may find he or she can't just follow the crowd; the situation requires action on his or her own. Then too, relying on others to develop alternatives, your child diminishes the opportunity to develop the necessary skills for coming up with appropriate personal alternatives. That means your child will tend to let others exert control over his or her own actions, which lessens the chances of satisfying his or her own unique needs and wants.

And then there are those times when the obvious solution to a problem sets your child up for more than he or she can handle.

> Carmen, an eighth-grade student, ambitiously decided she was going to improve her grades from an average C level to an A level. She began with a spurt of enthusiasm and increased effort, but within a few weeks felt discouraged and seemed about to abandon her goal. Her parents, seeing her frustration, suggested she reevaluate her goal. She had clearly underestimated the things she'd have to do to make the improvement desired. After some discussion and a fresh look at where her greatest difficulty lay, they agreed that a more immediate realistic goal would be to work on improving her English grades. Working on her English skills could have a spill-over effect, improving reading speed and comprehension and also her ability to handle writing assignments and essay exams. At the end of the next marking period, Carmen recorded her first B in English, and she'd raised her history grade as well.

In Carmen's situation, it was both a question of clarifying what she wanted in terms of her ability and then discovering a practical route to a realistic goal.

Keep this example in mind. It's a good illustration of the fact that decision skills work to make things easier. As parents, we often tend to chide children for taking the easy way out—for shortcutting the decision process. What you really want to point out is that doing so only *seems* the easy way out. Often it sets one up for greater difficulties ahead. Applying decision skills often saves a youngster the frustration of working toward objectives that are not realistic. When objectives are not realistic, the search for a way to achieve them becomes impossible.

Helping your child learn to develop feasible alternatives is easily done in everyday family interactions. It's a simple matter of getting your child to tune into possibilities in the world around him or her, then getting him or her to adopt a consistent line of approach to exploring those. Decisions about family trips, curfew, earning money, social activities, etc. lend themselves naturally to a consideration of alternatives. Discuss local or national news events in the context of how you or your child might think a situation could be handled. Even the simplest things—deciding what clothes to wear, what chores to do first, what to watch on TV—can provide valuable learning experiences.

Help your child take advantage of all these opportunities. Show him or her that the basic steps for developing alternatives apply and make good sense in any situation. Use simple examples to advantage—they allow you to illustrate the point without your child's getting nervous that what you're really trying to do is control his or her alternatives. (Remember that sensitivity about independence!) Point out how the process works in nonthreatening situations. Here, for example, is how the steps for developing alternatives look when going out to eat:

1. *State the decision:* What shall I eat?
2. *Determine what you want to happen:* I want something I've never had, but it must not include something I know I don't like, e.g. garlic.
3. *List alternatives you know about:* What's on the menu that looks new to me?

4. *Identify sources for developing other alternatives:* Ask the waiter about specials; ask him or have him ask the chef which dishes are prepared with garlic.

5. *Add new alternatives to those you are considering:* Is there a dish incorporating garlic so subtly that the taste is masked? Is a familiar dish perhaps prepared a new way here?

I'm not suggesting you run your child through a litany every time some matter of choice arises. Just coach your child into asking a series of fairly routine questions when he or she is up against a choice of what to do.

- What do I have to decide?
- What do I want?
- What do I know I could do to get it?
- How can I find out if there might be something else I could do?
- What about other possibilities?

The questions correspond to the steps for developing alternatives. You don't even have to ask your child to memorize them. When your child mentions a decision that faces him or her, you can simply get into the habit of asking these questions during the course of conversation. They're nonthreatening, and they clearly help provide an approach to what he or she has to do to reach a decision. Before long your child will have incorporated these questions into his or her own repertory of responses to the challenges posed in reaching for goals.

The process is an easy, natural one, but it does take thought to carry through. You'll probably need to help from time to time. Your child may not be clear about values or value priorities; he or she may not know where to turn to develop new alternatives. Often, all it takes to start your child in the right direction is to have him or her develop a list of possibilities and identify what brought them to mind.

Margie regularly complained of how bored she was. She was tired of doing the same old things. Whenever her parents asked her what she'd rather do, she either shrugged and muttered, "I don't know—something different," or she'd speak vaguely of going somewhere where there would be other things to do. Finally her parents pointed out to her that this was a decision situation—she could either choose to explore possibilities that might be available or settle for things as they were. Her complaining only masked the fact that she was choosing not to take responsibility for change. They suggested she make up a list of possibilities, together with a note of what made her think of each. Her initial list was short, but it included mention of two possibilities she'd thought of as a result of what friends had mentioned. Her mother then suggested her friends might be able to provide other ideas, as well as give her some sense of what would be involved in the alternatives she'd already listed.

Building skills here will almost always prove easier if you get your child to tune into resources he or she is familiar with first. Those often of themselves will lead to the consideration of other possibilities. However, in this context, be alert to any evident tendency to turn only to particular sources when developing alternatives. In Margie's case, if she's a girl easily influenced by peers when deciding what to do, it might profit to point out that her alternatives list is heavily dependent on what she sees her friends doing. Maybe the problem is that she's bored because she's following others' leads too consistently instead of checking things out further for herself.

### Learning to Assess Risks and Consequences

Young people take risks all the time. In most cases they do not bother to assess or anticipate risks because they do things without taking consequences fully into account beforehand.

Risk has to do with the consequences of an action. In specific, it is the likelihood of an outcome occurring as a result of action taken. Every choice has *at least* one consequence and may very well have several. Each consequence has a certain chance or probability attached to it. That's something children purport to understand, but their understanding is usually only partial, focused primarily or exclusively on the obvious and failing to take in the total picture.

> Mitchell found English a difficult, dull subject. His teacher in the ninth grade was fairly easygoing, giving tests and report assignments on a predictable basis. Mitchell observed that the teacher was not particularly attentive to students during tests and would accept completed report assignments without much question about whether they were students' original work. He knew that school policy dictated an automatic F for students caught cheating but also saw that the chances of getting caught were relatively slight. Weighing that risk only, Mitchell relied on cheating to get through his ninth-grade English class with an acceptable grade.

Of course you could fault the teacher in this situation, but the point is that Mitchell's actions carry other consequences he probably isn't taking into account at all. He misses what opportunity exists to improve skills in an area where he is deficient. He may find he can't keep up in the tenth grade unless he relies on the same strategy, and the longer the strategy continues, the greater the risk that eventually he will be found out. If he has any aspirations in the direction of higher education, he may compromise those through his failure to develop prerequisite skills for admission into college.

It isn't just this kind of decision that has consequences beyond those the youngster may be taking into account at the moment. All kinds of decisions have risks attached to them, including decisions that don't on the surface appear to involve a risk of anything negative happening as a result.

The following decisions are typical for the junior high age group. Each has a possible set of consequences attached to it, and there's some risk involved in each case—that is, that an undesired consequence will come about.

- Deciding to go out for a sport instead of having free time after school.

- Deciding not to argue with parents about when to come home at night.
- Deciding to sneak around to see friends one's parents don't like.
- Deciding to experiment with alcohol or marijuana.
- Deciding to drop a friend who is being made fun of by other kids.

It doesn't take but a moment to see that each of these decisions could have positive and negative outcomes. Yes, even the decision to experiment with marijuana could have positive outcomes—anything from greater peer acceptance to satisfying once and for all the curiosity about what it's like to be high. (Not everybody likes the feeling.)

The problem with youngsters is that they tend to jump at an action without considering the whole range of possible consequences and so are never fully aware of the risks involved. Experimentation with alcohol or drugs is a good example. One possible outcome is that the child will continue to use them. In fact, about one in ten high school students is a frequent drug user, and alcoholism is increasingly a problem among teenagers as well. So a lot of experimentation can lead to continued use or chronic dependence, a risk the first-time experimenter often does not consider.

But let's not stick with just a "worst cases" focus. What about the decision to go out for a sport? Ask your child to list what he or she feels the consequences of that decision might be. Then compare his or her list with the list that follows (which isn't necessarily complete).

*Positive Consequences*

Regular opportunity to indulge in an enjoyable activity
Be part of a team and learn value of teamwork
Develop good physical condition
Win the admiration of peers
Meet new friends

Give an outlet to competitive spirit
Represent the school in contests with other schools
Learn greater self-discipline

*Negative Consequences*

Unable to keep up with school assignments
Less time with nonparticipating friends
Unable to keep up with chores around the home
Less time with family
Injury
Pressure to perform from others
Humiliation at moments of poor performance/loss
Won't make the team; just sit on the bench

Chances are, if your child is at all considering going out for a team, he or she has focused on the obvious positives for the most part. Your child may take some of the more obvious negative possibilities into account, but he or she probably hasn't listed more than one or two. He or she probably has an easy answer to any question about risk—typically, "Don't worry, Mom and Dad. I'll keep up my grades." Children this age very commonly assume that all it takes to avoid negative consequences is positively stated intentions. They don't often sit down to figure out what the actual element of risk is and how to work around that.

Adolescents, because of their concern to be independent, tend not to refer to their parents as readily as younger children. That can be frustrating in the context of trying to help them make reasoned decisions in fairly routine situations. It can be alarming when it comes to some of the more difficult decisions common at this age. If your child does not tell you what's going on in his or her life, you'll be hard put to provide guidance when it may be most needed. Here's where establishing trust pays off.

At this stage, you want as much interaction as possible when it comes to discussing consequences. To get an idea of how your child is likely to respond to a risk-packed situation, complete the disclosure profile below. In each of the dilemmas presented, where do you think your child would be *most likely* to go for help? Check only one column for each situation.

### Disclosure Profile

| To whom would your child turn to if . . . | Acquaintance | Close Friend | Sibling | Parent | Self |
|---|---|---|---|---|---|
| Caught cheating on a test? | _____ | _____ | _____ | _____ | _____ |
| He or she wanted to know something about sex? | _____ | _____ | _____ | _____ | _____ |
| A friend needed help with a drug problem? | _____ | _____ | _____ | _____ | _____ |
| He or she wanted ideas about what to do on weekends? | _____ | _____ | _____ | _____ | _____ |
| He or she felt left out and neglected? | _____ | _____ | _____ | _____ | _____ |
| His or her friends were doing something that bothered him or her? | _____ | _____ | _____ | _____ | _____ |

If you think your child would turn to you in most of these situations, then you are a member of a fortunate but small group. Most junior high students would go to their friends for help in these situations. While it's okay to use friends for help, the young teenager is not always the best source of information about consequences attached to serious decisions and the real risks associated with them.

If you have doubts about whom your child would most likely refer to, ask. But avoid a direct confrontation in which you make it clear you expect your child to come to you. Rather, weave your question into an incident of mutual interest. For example, ask how he or she would go about trying to help a friend who was shoplifting. Don't give your child the feeling you are prying or giving him or her the third degree. Stay away from telling your child what he or she should do. You want to communicate a natural concern about a situation that has serious consequences. You also want to gauge how comfortable your child feels talking about this kind of thing with you. If the answers you hear show your child is in a hurry to change the subject, chances are he or she doesn't see you as the first person to turn to for guidance in difficult decision matters. To bring about a change here, you've got to convince your child of your concern and win his or her trust that you won't step in to impose your priorities on him or her when it comes to providing guidance. Refer to pages 123–129 for guidelines to help you here.

In addition to determining where your child is likely to turn for help with his or her difficult decisions, it's also important you gain a sense of how your child views consequences. Does he or she care about them? When does he or she care? One way to check out your child's perceptions is to review some of the consequences you have established in the home or that you know have been established in school. Test his or her awareness. Is your child aware of the consequences of :

- Being caught stealing?
- Doing unsatisfactory schoolwork?
- Disobeying a parent or teacher?
- Losing a piece of personal property?
- Damaging the property of another person?
- Coming home late?
- Fighting with another person?
- Failing to do chores that are his or her responsibility?
- Running through his or her allowance as soon as he or she gets it?
- Being found using drugs or alcohol?

It's in recognizing the consequences attached to actions like these that your child begins to develop the skills necessary to anticipate consequences existing in situations not covered in the normal activities of home or school. You've made great progress as a parent if you get your child to start thinking about what might happen, before he or she embarks on a course of action. Is your child realistically taking risks into account as well as looking toward the immediate gain he or she hopes for or expects?

The final thing to consider in connection with all this is: When does your child think it worthwhile to risk negative consequences? Where consequences are loosely constructed, arbitrary, or rarely enforced, it is probably easier to take chances. Likewise, when the immediate payoff appears terrific, a child might decide to risk the consequences because it seems worth it—a party may be so terrific he or she won't mind being grounded for the next ten days for coming home late. Most adults can easily relate to a youngster's special pleasure in occasionally flouting known consequences in order to satisfy the desires of the moment.

Unfortunately, allowing a focus on immediate pleasure or gain to take over too often means blocking out any consideration of risks for damage over the long term. Look back at the example previously given of Mitchell, easily making it through a subject by cheating. He obviously hasn't considered the whole picture.

It isn't always easy to teach children to understand that there are long-term as well as immediate consequences for most acts and that nothing is worth the risk until both short- and long-term implications have been considered. One very effective way to get a child to begin thinking situations through more completely is to subject decisions that haven't worked out to review.

I've devised a "fault tree" model that points children into consideration of consequences across a broader spectrum than just immediate goals, using use the example we started with earlier—Mitchell cheating his way through ninth-grade English.

**The Fault Tree**

Decision Situation: Whether or not to cheat on English tests

*Yes: Possible Outcomes (as seen by Mitchell)*
1. Get caught and receive F grade
2. Get away with it and pass

*No: Possible Outcomes (as seen by Mitchell)*
1. Have to study boring, difficult subject
2. Might get low grade or fail

*Risks*
Yes-1: Not likely—teacher inattentive
Yes-2: Likely—easy to do
No-1: Likely—don't enjoy subject
No-2: Likely—not good at English
↓
*Decision:* Decide to cheat on tests
*Result:* Passed ninth-grade English with no problem
*Worth it?* Yes
↓
*Things Overlooked*

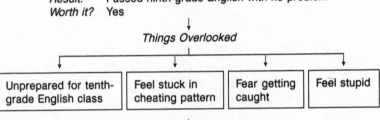

| Unprepared for tenth-grade English class | Feel stuck in cheating pattern | Fear getting caught | Feel stupid |

↓
*Decision worth it? No!*

This model provides a good way to help young people review actions that have backfired on them. It graphically illustrates the reality of consequences that extend beyond the moment or that develop as a result after immediate, transitory goals have been met.

You can also adapt the model to use for present situations that provide your child a difficult choice. In that case, have your child sketch out the decision in terms of what seems to him or her to be the immediate outcomes possible. Ask what your child feels his or her decision would be based on his or her perception of these and his or her sense of the risks involved. Then, have your child think ahead to what his or her situation will be subsequently, *after* the initial goal has been achieved. What long-term effect may come into play? How will your child feel about any changes that may come about as a result of reaching immediately for the benefit he or she sees in the short run? Is he or she prepared for more than just the short-range consequences?

When using the fault tree to help your child pinpoint omissions when looking at consequences, remember that the objective is to have your child recognize them. Don't use this as a kind of parental "I told you so!" Don't sketch it out for your child as a means of showing him or her what he or she should have done or what you're convinced should be done now. Always keep in mind that your objective is responsible independence over the long term. In following through on this exercise, as well as others in this book, be alert to the reality that you, too, must distinguish between short-term and long-term consequences: the transitory satisfaction of getting your child to do what you want the way you think it should be done now and the longer-lasting achievement of teaching your child how to make and evaluate decisions on his or her own.

# 15

# "Where Do I Go From Here?" —Senior High

The high school teenager stands on the brink, poised between childhood dependence and adult independence, faced with decisions that have lifelong implications and yet so often totally preoccupied with just the concerns of the moment. The normal youngster at this age is a living paradox. Teenagers reflect a variety of seemingly contradictory attitudes and characteristics. They are both:

- impulsive and thoughtful
- shy and confident
- rude and sensitive
- daring and cautious
- individualistic and conforming
- arrogant and timid
- tough and scared
- omnipotent-feeling and powerless
- mature and childish

It's no wonder parents anticipate these years with anxiety and fear, and it's easy to see why they so often feel exasperated.

Suddenly a whole bunch of conflict-charged situations arise. Issues relating to teenage sexuality, preparation for college or work, the first car, financial independence, and treatment as a young adult virtually explode into the family setting.

On top of this, the high school teenager experiences his or her first hard confrontation with the consequences of past action. Past performance is evaluated for evidence of future possibilities. Poor grades affect college options, a lack of salable skills hinders the chance to make money, and previous labeling, once so easily accepted, seems to get in the way even when he or she wants to make a fresh start. All of this is coupled with a compelling, often desperate search for self-discovery—"Who am I?"

During these years teenagers may rationalize the anxiety they naturally experience with the complaint "nobody understands me," somehow faulting the world around them for their feelings of dislocation. But that is only a handy excuse for refusing to move ahead purposefully. Relying on it will only compromise a teenager's struggle for mature independence. Refusing to meet the challenge of obstacles facing him or her, whatever they may be, will only lead to choices in which he or she settles for less than the best.

### WHAT'S A PARENT TO DO?

Your task at this stage is to get your child ready to take control of his or her own life. These are the years in which it all has to pull together. Your child's decision skills should be fairly well developed by now. He or she should have a reasonably clear idea about what his or her values and value priorities are, what long-term goals he or she wants to focus on, how to go about developing alternatives, and what to do in anticipating consequences and weighing risks.

Your energies should be focused on helping and supporting efforts to put skills to work. What you specifically do will depend on your child's needs. You will find yourself concentrating on different things at different times, depending on the situations faced and your child's ability to cope with the demands they present. In general, you'll be working to ensure an adult orientation to:

- *Planning,* so that your child faces choices about the future in advance as much as possible. The idea is to have your child take advantage of opportunities, rather than wait with action until a crisis develops or circumstances force a choice from limited options.
- *Self-awareness,* so that your child has a realistic sense of his or her own capabilities. You want your child to feel capable of influencing his or her own future, that he or she can overcome limitations and work around setbacks. But you also want your child to recognize that there are limits to what is possible, that at times he or she will have to compromise ideal goals in order to move at least somewhat closer to what he or she wants.
- *Flexibility,* so that your child grasps the fact that decisions are not necessarily irreversible, realizing that he or she can change goals and adjust actions when this proves desirable or necessary. It's also important your child tune into and learn to cope with the inconsistencies and uncertainties in the changing world around him or her.
- *Independence and interdependence,* so that your child understands what responsibilities he or she must assume for him- or herself, but also how those decisions impact on others and his or her relationships with others. At the same time, you want to prompt your child into inner-directed behavior, so that his or her actions truly reflect personal priorities rather than just echo others' expectations of him or her.

The teen years provide you the last sure chance to help move your child to mature self-sufficiency. Now more than ever your focus is on the future, a future that looms increasingly near. You'll still be faced with present realities, behavior that is or isn't acceptable in the context of the moment. But your concern about that behavior will increasingly be in terms of its implications for the future. What does it show about your teenager's readiness to take charge of his or her own destiny? How will your response help ensure your child adopts a pattern of behavior that provides him or her the best chance of getting what he or she wants out of life?

Parents face the same dilemma with high school teenagers that they have to face up to with younger adolescents—a tendency on the child's part to emphasize independence from parental "interference." You see your teenager struggling with unfamiliar situations and trying to develop an orientation to the future. Because you have experience with things your child is encountering for the first time, you're certain you can provide meaningful guidance. You can mention things to watch out for, suggest lines of action that will avoid or overcome difficulties that may threaten. But your teenager doesn't seem to want to hear it. He or she is convinced your experiences have only a limited applicability to the present; your teenager is certain you have little idea of his or her needs and priorities.

You have to tread carefully if you are to be of help to your child. You have to keep lines of communication open. You have to accept that at this point you must rely more on your child to take and sustain initiatives. You can't expect to protect your child by making decisions for him or her or to provide guidance by telling your child what to do. You have to trust your child's ability to make more—eventually all—of his or her own decisions.

The truth is, young people generally have a fairly good idea of what they want. Most of them, in fact, want pretty much what you think they should want. In a recent survey put together by teenagers and sponsored by the Population Institute, teenage girls indicated their goal preferences to be "getting a job I enjoy," "preparing for the future," "making it on my own," "getting good grades," and "getting along with my family." Having children ranked tenth, getting married ranked fourteenth, being popular ranked sixteenth, and getting high and hanging out ranked seventeenth out of seventeen. Boys listed their preferences in the same order except for stressing "making money" where girls indicated "getting along with my family." Having fun ranked twelfth, getting married sixteenth, and getting high and hanging out was again dead last at seventeenth. While this is only one study, most research confirms that teenagers in general have values and goals very similar to those of the adult population.

Then why are there so many problems at this stage?

Because teenagers typically have trouble developing an approach for getting what they want. They're facing adult choices for the first time, with only childhood experience to draw on. They feel helpless without daring to admit it, presented with a world of overwhelming choices they've never had to face before. Adding to their feelings of helplessness is the now inescapable realization of the awesome consequences that can result if they flub the big decisions of the high school years—sex, college, career, alcohol, drugs, friends.

The most effective help a parent can provide is to direct the teenager to use of the decision framework when it comes to handling choices. Your child has to learn how to analyze situations he or she encounters, to work out how to bypass pitfalls and surmount barriers that would otherwise keep achievable goals beyond reach.

Your task will be a lot easier if you've already begun to introduce your child to the basic skills involved in making good choices. If you haven't started the process, it's still not too late. You'll just have to work that much harder.


### Is Your Child Losing Control?

While you'll still exercise parental authority during the teen years, the appropriate progression is for your youngster to make more and more of his or her own decisions. As a family member, your child will still have to be guided by the family philosophy. But as an individual, he or she will increasingly take over the direction of his or her own life—course and career focuses in school, choice of friends and social patterns, leisure pursuits, romantic interests, etc.

There's great potential for confusion and trouble in all this. Your child, in seeking independently to establish his or her sense of direction, makes the appalling discovery that there are an infinite number of directions to go and seemingly only vague and occasional signposts to go by. One seems at a perpetual crossroads.

Children characteristically think of life settling into some kind of predictable order once they become adults. But then they reach the teen years and disillusion sets in. Decisions don't lead to happy endings; they lead to other decisions. Happiness isn't what comes after you've acted; it's how you feel as you act. These realizations are disillusioning because children instinctively view adulthood as the resolution of childhood, as a time when confusion, uncertainty, and a feeling of being powerless give way to clarity, certainty, and sure control. Just as they see themselves on the threshold of that resolution, it disappears, like a mirage. The world is still a place of mystery and a more ominous place of danger than ever.

The emphasis in this period must be on equipping your teenager to take responsible control of his or her own life. Positive follow-through requires your child to assume more control now. The big question is: Will your child be able to handle it? Will the shock of disillusion be something he or she can take in stride? The answer is almost certainly *yes* for the most part, but sometimes *no*.

As you observe your teenager, look for signs that he or she may be losing control. You'll recognize them by their negativity and by their characteristic downward spiral. Things to look out for include:

- A significant drop in school performance
- Increased friction and turmoil between you and your child

- A friendless existence marked by more time at home and increased feelings of loneliness
- Apparent boredom and lack of interest and involvement in much of anything
- More physical complaints, with little evidence of actual physical problems
- Less communication

You can't always count on your child to tell you things are out of control. For one thing, he or she may not fully recognize that's the case. After all, this is his or her first try at many things. Your child is not altogether sure what it means to be "in control." Then too, teenagers don't like the humiliation of admitting they can't handle their affairs as well as they expected to.

> Beverly was increasingly at odds with her mother regarding her boyfriend, Spencer. Spencer was a carelessly handsome, temperamental seventeen-year-old who was frequently in trouble for cutting school to hang out with a group of older teens who liked getting high. Beverly's mother was dismayed one evening to see her daughter come home with a black eye that Spencer had given her. She expressed immediate concern and alarm, whereupon Beverly burst into tears, screaming at her mother, "You don't understand! You never understand! Why can't you just once get off my back!" Her mother was left in a state of shock.

A teenager's parents can expect to have their patience pushed to the limit. Just when they think they've experienced the ultimate in exasperation and are about to explode with their own anger, they must show love. Just when they feel they're ready to throw in the towel, more than ever they have to stick to limits and enforce consequences.

Your child may at times appear to be rejecting you and everything you stand for—and sometimes will be. Nevertheless, home and family provide an indispensable haven from the rest of the confusing world. Believe it or not, that yelling, irrational ingrate needs you very much. Venting frustrations is something your child needs to do now and then.

What! Do I mean a parent should just sit back and take it? No, I don't. What I mean is that the parent's response should fit the needs of the situation, not make it worse than it already is.

You *can* express your feelings of frustration and anger. It's perfectly appropriate for you to describe how you feel and why. But do that as calmly as possible and always in the context of showing that you care, that you want to help, that you are willing to be supportive. Observe these suggestions for maximum effectiveness in helping your child maintain/regain control:

- *Always show love and support,* even in the most difficult situations. However, don't suppress your other feelings. Keep in mind that your child has to learn to deal with the fact of others' sometimes feeling that perhaps he or she is not reliable or even likable in certain situations.
- *Keep communication lines open.* Don't shut your child out. Don't let your child shut you out either. Insist on discussion of situations that clearly require response or adjustment of behavior if worse difficulties are to be avoided later.
- *Clarify and stick to limits and consequences.* Saying *no* is at times the clearest message that you care about what's happening with your child.
- *Take your child's problems seriously.* Some may appear ridiculous, even laughable to you. If they're evidently serious as far as your child is concerned, treat them that way.
- *Don't wait for problems to develop* or for a crisis to come to a head. If you have a hunch or suspicion that something is going wrong, take action.
- *Keep things in perspective.* Don't jump to the immediate conclusion that the fact of a problem—even a serious

problem—reflects your child's total inability to handle responsibility. Don't minimize difficulties either, but remember, there have undoubtedly been times when *you* haven't seemed or been in control.

On a skill level, (re)gaining control requires a focus in three areas. (You are, of course, building on the foundation of a whole range of skills developed over the past years.)

*1.* Learning to be specific about values and then using those values as standards for making judgments throughout the decision process.

*2.* Knowing how to find, evaluate, and utilize information effectively.

*3.* Evaluating alternatives and their potential consequences in order to identify the best course of action in any critical situation.

The balance of this chapter will be devoted to promoting your ability to help and provide support in each of these areas.

### USING VALUES IN THE TOTAL DECISION PROCESS

By now you recognize that values determine a person's goals and actions, as well as what risks he or she is willing to take. They make it possible for the decider to establish priorities. As your teenager gets specific about his or her values and value priorities, he or she reduces the work required when new decisions are faced.

In the previous chapter I presented a value inventory to use for helping junior high–age youngsters begin to get a sense of values and value priorities. That exercise is also a valuable one for older teenagers. But now add in an additional consideration: What evidence will be required in order for your child to feel he or she has attained or affirmed the value indicated? (You can use those listed and/or others you think relevant.)

## When Do You Know You've Attained What's Important?

| Value | Very important | Somewhat important | Not important | Evidence of attainment |
|---|---|---|---|---|
| Independence | _____ | _____ | _____ | _____ |
| Friendship | _____ | _____ | _____ | _____ |
| Good family relations | _____ | _____ | _____ | _____ |
| Job satisfaction | _____ | _____ | _____ | _____ |
| Physical appearance | _____ | _____ | _____ | _____ |
| Feeling useful | _____ | _____ | _____ | _____ |
| Happiness | _____ | _____ | _____ | _____ |
| Career success | _____ | _____ | _____ | _____ |
| Winning | _____ | _____ | _____ | _____ |
| Giving and receiving love | _____ | _____ | _____ | _____ |
| Privacy | _____ | _____ | _____ | _____ |
| Learning | _____ | _____ | _____ | _____ |
| Leadership | _____ | _____ | _____ | _____ |
| Self-expression | _____ | _____ | _____ | _____ |
| Recognition | _____ | _____ | _____ | _____ |
| Grades | _____ | _____ | _____ | _____ |

You can collect this information through the normal give and take you have with your child every day, or you can actually have him or her fill in the blanks here. Whatever the procedure, the information is critical for indicating what's required for attaining certain priorities. As your child faces decisions relating to school performance, what to do after high school, job opportunities, or relationships, he or she gets a clear sense of what is really meant when something is termed important (i.e., valued). Once that meaning is established, it becomes much easier to see what targets for future achievement make sense and why. Your child will be able to home in on targets more easily, too.

Once your teenager has clarified values this way, the logical next step is to project him- or herself into the future. This is a good way to introduce a perspective that goes beyond the moment. It prompts an evaluation of decision possibilities in light of a contemplated choice of action—anything from dropping out of school to getting married or enlisting for military service.

### Lifestyle Projection

| What I want | One year from now | Five years from now |
|---|---|---|
| Where I'll live | | |
| Who my friends will be | | |
| What I'll be doing (work or school) | | |
| Accomplishments by this time | | |
| Family situation | | |
| New skills developed | | |
| Financial status | | |
| People who will influence me | | |
| How I'll spend my free time | | |

A lifestyle projection is a good way to test alternatives in a decision situation. Basically that's accomplished by asking, "Assuming I pursue this option, where will I be one year from now; where will I be five years from now?" That requires immediately facing practical follow-through considerations: "How good are my chances of getting where I want to be in the time given?" "What will I have to do next to move closer to my long-term goals?" "Would a different choice now improve my chances for satisfaction later?"

Fred told his parents he'd decided not to go to college. He felt he'd rather pursue his interest in automobiles and take an auto mechanics course offered at a nearby vocational school. His father, a college graduate, was appalled. He told Fred his decision was a serious mistake. Auto mechanics offered no future. If Fred planned on throwing his life away in this fashion, he needn't ask for help later once he found he couldn't make ends meet. And he'd have to finance his vocational school training himself. He could not expect his parents to make the kind of investment in this dead-end pursuit that they would have been willing to make in a college education.

Too many parents show concern for their teenager's future by projecting their own vision of what that will be. They fear their child's priorities are short-sighted; they're convinced that in the long run their child will see the wisdom of their approach to the future. So they make the very serious mistake of pushing their child in a direction he or she says he or she doesn't want to go.

It isn't necessarily that the parents will be wrong in their projection of what's likely to happen. Rather, the mistake lies in the approach they take to "helping" their teenager get a clearer focus. How do you suppose a young man like Fred feels at his father's putdown of his career goals? Even if his father proves more realistic than Fred in the long run, he hasn't really helped and supported his son's efforts to plan his own future. Eventually Fred does have to get a grip on how to do that. He is going to have to take responsibility for his own life choices.

Pushing a child in the direction you think he or she should go is a far cry from guiding your child to a choice that works for him or her, even if in the long run it turns out to be the same choice. Fred's father would do a lot better to prompt Fred himself into questioning the wisdom of his decision. One of two things could happen:

1. Fred discovers that his assumptions about a future in auto mechanics are unrealistic and decides to explore other options that position him more favorably for achievement of long-range goals. He rethinks his decision not to go to college.

2. Fred discovers that auto mechanics can lead to opportuni-

ties to get what he wants from a career, provided he follows a specific line of focus that is now more clear to him.

Yes, Fred still might wind up going the route of auto mechanics, but if so, he'll follow that route with a clearer sense of the potential there and a heightened awareness of what it takes to achieve that potential. The question for Fred's father at that point will be whether he's really willing to accept that Fred has priorities of his own when it comes to what to do with his life. Parenting toward independence implies parental acceptance of a child's right to determine his or her own future, even when choices do not reflect priorities the parent might have wished to see emphasized.

Concentrate on ensuring your child makes a well-considered choice with maximum awareness of its implications for the future. Don't try to push your child into reaching for your vision of his or her future. Get your child to evaluate the potential for satisfaction in what he or she does. Encourage your child to:

- Dream a little. Get your child to devise as clear an answer as possible to the question "How is this going to work out?"
- Respond to what he or she wants, not to what you and/or your child's friends would like him or her to want.
- Evaluate his or her life experiences to get a true feeling of what provides personal satisfaction and a sense of self-worth.
- Stay attuned to his or her own uniqueness.
- Anticipate what might block progress en route to goals he or she has set.
- Adjust goals whenever new information indicates an area of previous oversight with respect to potential problems or opportunities.
- Stick up for his or her own choices.

### IDENTIFYING, EVALUATING, AND USING
### INFORMATION

Sometimes it seems we are in an age of information overload. There is so much information around to use when making decisions that it can seem too much to handle.

Elaine, a high school honors student, had chosen a college preparatory curriculum with the clear intention of continuing her education after graduating from high school. At the beginning of her senior year, she sent away for college catalogs to discover what schools offered the best programs in areas she was interested in. But by December it was evident she had failed to narrow down her range of choices. She put off sending in admission applications until finally her parents grew concerned. "I don't know which school to apply to," she protested as they applied pressure for her to make up her mind. "They all seem to offer something I'm interested in." They warned her that further delay could compromise her chances for admission anywhere, then pushed her into applying at least to her mother's alma mater, a school they were confident would accept her readily and provide her some program in line with her capabilities.

Decisions can be held up by an inability to sift through and process information as well as by an absence of sufficient information for understanding alternatives available. In either case, unless a person develops a viable approach to satisfying information needs (and those include information-management needs), he or she will have difficulty reaching a decision. Often that leads to last-minute decisions made under pressure; often it means letting others take the initiative in making the decision that has to be made.

You'll want to make sure this doesn't happen with your child. Letting others decide provides an easy excuse for copping out. After all, it wasn't his or her idea, was it? It also tends to lessen the commitment with which your child follows through on the course of action selected.

You can provide a lot of assistance in this area. Get your

child to take advantage of the information resources available. Look for books and other publications that can help establish a sense of direction. What references exist for clarifying the important issues that come up in connection with the critical decision areas for this age—job opportunities and occupation choices, teen sexuality, college, lifestyle orientation, etc.? Identify people who might have good information. Tie present considerations in with past experience.

It's not that you should do all the work. Rather, you want to get a good idea yourself of possibilities in areas of concern. You want to be able to guide your child to resources that could help him or her get a clearer understanding of possibilities relating to his or her interests and priorities.

In line with this, one of your first aid-and-support tasks is to find out what your teenager's information needs are. Ask questions, with particular emphasis on your child's awareness of personal priorities and the implications of following through with action to promote them. If your child has trouble responding, if he or she just plain doesn't know what to say, you'll know he or she needs help. The same will apply if the answers provided are too vague or self-contradictory to serve as guidelines for achieving goals. Get your child to respond to questions that occur to you, making it clear all the while that your concern is that the answers he or she comes up with serve *his or her* interests best. Let your child know you're prepared to accept a reasoned decision that realistically takes risks and consequences into account. You're not just trying to get him or her to do things as you would do them if the choice were yours.

Your concern here shouldn't be exercised only in the context of your teenager's deciding what to do with his or her life. It's equally important your child know what he or she is about when it comes to setting and following through on priorities relating more explicitly to present wants and needs.

Sixteen-year-old Brenda obtained her parents' assent to a party to be held at home for a group of about twenty friends. But then she asked in addition that they allow wine and beer to be served, since this was "routine" at other parties she'd attended. Her parents were uncomfortable with her request, as well as somewhat alarmed at the news that alcohol was being served at other teen parties. They did not think it appropriate to serve alcoholic beverages to underage youngsters. However, they knew this party was important to Brenda and wanted it to be a success for her.

A lot of parents would feel themselves caught in a dilemma here, drawing a surface connection between success and allowing alcohol to be served. They'd fall into viewing the situation in terms of how their child presented it to them. An alert parent will realize there are information gaps to be filled here: What does Brenda most associate with success in this situation? Is her priority getting people together for enjoyable social interaction or is it throwing a "blast" event that requires stimulants beyond good social interaction? Will all her friends make attendance conditional on alcohol availability? Isn't there a good chance that some of them would feel more comfortable at an alcohol-free party? Many young people appreciate not having to perform a certain way to show their supposed sophistication or ability to handle alcohol. Good food in good quantity plus good music and a welcoming atmosphere are often enough to guarantee success. And then, what about the possibility of things getting out of hand?

All these are information points that Brenda should be attentive to for developing a good sense of alternatives and consequences in this situation. And that's not even to go into the question of resolving a value conflict with her parents on the point of teenage drinking.

Brenda's parents told her serving alcohol at a party for underage young people was not something they could condone. They pointed out that this would clearly violate limits established in the family philosophy. They questioned the connection she was drawing between success and the availability of alcoholic beverages and suggested she investigate other possibilities for ensuring her guests enjoyed themselves. They agreed to help her with food and entertainment arrangements once she had a clearer view of other options available.

Whether it's a matter of career planning or planning a party, help your child develop a list of options. Help him or her think through the implications of each—not by telling your child what will or should happen, but by querying his or her understanding of possible risks and how to take these into account. As options are rejected, explore the reasons for rejection. You'll soon discover where faulty connections are being made because of information oversights that should be corrected.

Keep a list of possible alternatives and why your child favors or rejects them. If it's a career choice, note occupations under consideration; if it's a party choice, note activities of potential interest. Does your teenager's list show a tendency to think in stereotypes? Does your child, for example, see career opportunities in education as limited to teaching in the public school system? Does he or she view parties merely in limited terms of eating, drinking, and dancing?

Encourage a brainstorming session for other possibilities in areas to which he or she is taking only a "once over lightly" approach. What about consumer education possibilities? What about educational publishing? What about renting a teen film favorite for part of a party's entertainment? What about putting on a talent show? Get your child to look beyond the limits of his or her everyday view of the world. Once she or he is turned on to a possibility that excites him or her, that will provide a further impetus for looking beyond seeming dilemmas posed by perception of only limited alternatives. Get your teenager to look into what he or she finds appealing or enjoyable in his or her everyday existence, too, for further clues to alternatives that don't appear obvious while thinking only in terms bounded by what seems to be expected by general convention.

Make sure your teenager is alert to the three areas of information need that come into play in making decisions:

*1.* Information about him- or herself—skills, values, goals, resources, likes and dislikes, attitudes, etc.

*2.* Information about the world around him or her—society's values and expectations, laws, economic realities, available opportunities, different beliefs and/or cultural orientations.

*3.* Information about alternative actions under consideration—feasibility, possible outcomes, risks involved, and steps to follow with in the event of either success or failure.

Information needs have not been satisfied until each of these three areas have been taken into consideration.

### FINDING THE VERY BEST ALTERNATIVE

Susan and Bill, both high school juniors, had been going together since the eighth grade. They were deeply in love, and their feelings led them to engage regularly in sexual relations. Worried about their situation and concerned to avoid trouble ahead, they realized a need to make some decisions about their relationship. Neither Bill nor Susan dared to admit the full extent of their intimacies to their parents, but when Bill spoke tentatively to his parents about possibly getting married soon, his parents suspected it might in large part be to resolve feelings of conflict about sexual intimacy.

How should Bill's parents have helped him work out the best alternative for response to this situation?

The most immediate thing to do in a situation like this is to play out possible alternatives. Would that entail pointedly confronting the kids about suspicions of sexual intimacy? It very easily could, but it needn't. Remember that the real point is to get Susan and Bill to tune in to the outcomes associated with various options. Confrontation may shift the focus of effort to either or both sides proving their sense of the situation somehow superior. Parent-child confrontation adds the risk that a power struggle will develop around the issue without really prompting a review of all the options. The sense of issue too easily shifts away from making a decision about sexuality in this case to demonstrating independence from parental control.

The process begins by pushing and stretching the decider's capacity for looking beyond the obvious outcomes. Bill and Susan are probably approaching the idea of marriage as a resolution of a present situation. They need to view it also in terms of the future it sets them up for. Marriage may seem to settle the problem that absorbs most of their attention right now, but it probably has the most severe implications when it comes to restricting subsequent opportunities either teenager still looks forward to—continuing education, choosing and pursuing a career objective, limiting the development of other relationships.

The parents must help the teenager develop a facility for predicting and comparing the full range of possible outcomes before a decision is made. The teenager's focus has to be pulled beyond immediate dilemmas, lest the eagerness or anxiety to resolve those lead to other equally or even more serious dilemmas.

Find out how good your child is when it comes to predicting and comparing outcomes. Discuss issues of interest to him or her: going to college, raising a family, dropping out of school, etc. Set up a hypothetical situation and get your teenager to respond to that. Whenever possible, turn his or her attention beyond concerns of the moment to considerations of the future as well. The exercise below poses a series of future-oriented considerations that can help stimulate your child's developing greater foresight.

With this exercise (you can vary the questions according to real or likely situations that concern you) come some obvious follow-up questions: How did you make your predictions? What information did you use? What did you learn about yourself? If you had to make a choice along any of these lines, what additional information would you like?

You can also encourage your child to take this approach to decision situations facing him or her now. Have your child

## Projecting Likely Outcomes

|  | Action | Outcome |
|---|---|---|

What if:

You did not go to college?

You never got married?

You joined the military service?

You worked in a factory?

You moved away from home?

You got married tomorrow?

You dropped out of high school?

You got pregnant?

You became a professional entertainer?

You had to support yourself tomorrow?

combine this exercise with the Lifestyle Projection exercise on page 258. How does your child see his or her decision affecting the likelihood of achieving goals anticipated there?

Once you see how your child makes predictions, you'll have a clearer sense of whether he or she is taking adequately into account each of the three information areas referred to above. You may also find that he or she tends to rely on certain information resources while overlooking others that could prove helpful in determining which alternative is indeed best. For example, teenagers sometimes seem determined to rely heavily on experience to satisfy information needs. Indeed, sometimes direct experience really does throw alternatives into very sharp focus. But adults know that it is not possible or even desirable to try to experience every alternative before making decisions about them. The teenager has to learn to predict outcomes via reliance on other information, too—observation of the experiences of others, reports of dangers or opportunities implicit in certain courses of action, etc.

Risk is always a key consideration. Any action involves some kind of risk, whether that's going for a drive, not setting an alarm, or engaging in sexual intimacies. It tends to influence people in one of two ways when not taken into account realistically: fear of risk often stops people from taking action to move from where they are to something with more promise; failure to take risk sufficiently into account often leads people to actions that backfire, keeping them from rather than bringing them closer to a goal they've been focusing on.

Risk has very little meaning except in association with specific alternatives and possible outcomes. And then it always has to be weighed against desirability factors. Something having a high risk potential may still represent the best choice because the desirability of the outcome aimed for seems worth the risk. In guiding your teenager into taking a realistic view of risks, the question is not always how to keep risks at an absolute minimum. Several questions are primary:

- What is the risk compared to the risks implicit in other alternatives?
- How does the risk compare with the desirability of the possible outcome?
- Is your child prepared to pay the price in the event of a failure to achieve the desired objective?

As you can see, answering these questions implies that the decider has done his or her homework to ensure as informed a selection of alternatives as possible, made with a clear awareness of how action to be taken accommodates value priorities and goals. In perhaps no other area of the decision process is more work required. Failure to do the work is evidence that a person is willing to settle for less than the best.

Let me reiterate once again that the best alternative for your child is not necessarily one you would have selected. That's to be expected; your child isn't you. Don't set as a test of his or her capabilities that your child follow your value priorities or pursue the goals you think he or she should be setting. When it comes to the alternative, ask yourself if your child has applied the decision framework fully. If so, then you can feel satisfied that you have done your job in providing the help and support he or she needed.

In the final analysis, your child's determination of what is the best alternative will stand up to scrutiny if:

- It is possible in terms of the resources available to your child.
- The payoff is consistent with your child's values and goals.
- The payoff is adequate as perceived by your child.
- Affairs can still be managed even if the worst possible thing happens.
- The impact on others is anticipated in advance.
- The decision has positive implications for your child's future.

In leading you through the various phases of childhood, we've now come full circle. It may seem strange for a moment to see that the teen years are not given as extensive a separate discussion as the earlier phases, particularly in view of the reality that the teen years so often present the most serious problems.

But there's another reality to take into account by this time. Your teenager is a budding adult. Although you retain a certain responsibility, your teenager now has to learn to accept accountability for his or her own choices. While it's appropriate that your teenager looks to you for guidance—and certainly he or she will continue to profit from your assistance and example—he or she is now at the point of taking the initiative when it comes to honing decisionmaking skills.

Now that you've seen your child to this age, direct him or her to the same resources you've used to come to an understanding of what goes into making good decisions. Refer your teenager to Part One of this book. The exercises you used to sharpen your awareness will serve him or her equally well. The procedures set out for your adoption are the same procedures he or she must follow to be assured of the best chance of reaching chosen goals.

This chapter is not really a conclusion. It is an introduction. It leads into the brief course in decisionmaking that you began with. It is further supplemented by the self-awareness exercises and commentary in Part Two. Share your reading of this book with your teenager. Help bring him or her to the realization that the best approach to be taken to present problems *and* opportunities is reliance on the decision framework. The payoffs are there for your teenager, too—involvement, control, freedom, and the sense of doing something worthwhile. Help your teenager see that from here on the shape of his or her life is a result of the decisions he or she makes. It's in your teenager's own best interests to make them as well as he or she can.

# Index